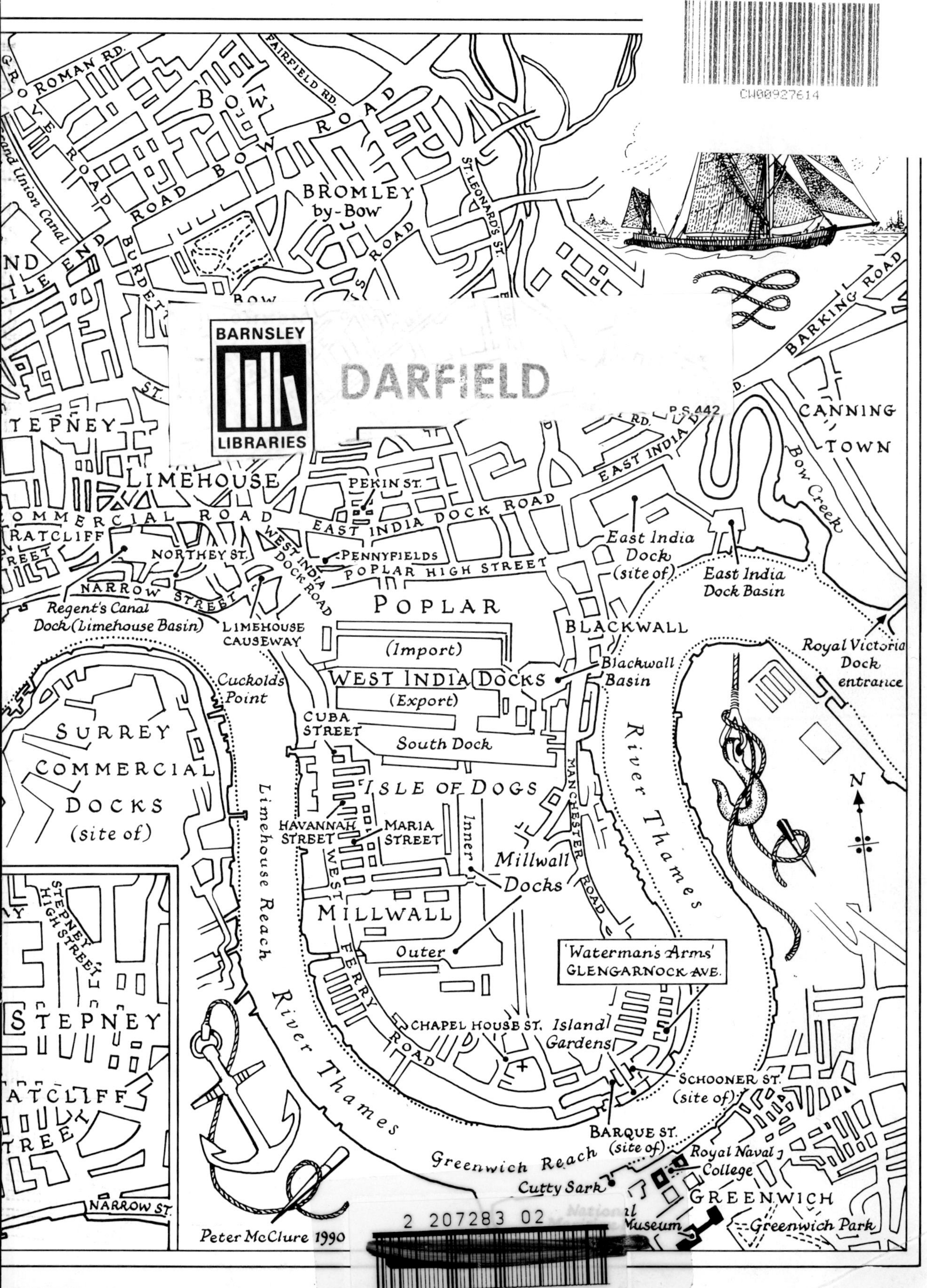
ROMAN RD.
FAIRFIELD RD.
BOW
BOW ROAD
ROAD
Grand Union Canal
BROMLEY by-Bow
ST. LEONARDS ST.
MILE END
BURDETT
BARKING ROAD
STEPNEY
LIMEHOUSE
COMMERCIAL ROAD
RATCLIFF
CANNING TOWN
Bow Creek
EAST INDIA DOCK ROAD
PEKIN ST.
WEST INDIA DOCK ROAD
NORTHEY ST.
PENNYFIELDS
POPLAR HIGH STREET
NARROW STREET
Regent's Canal Dock (Limehouse Basin)
LIMEHOUSE CAUSEWAY
POPLAR
East India Dock (site of)
East India Dock Basin
BLACKWALL
Royal Victoria Dock entrance
(Import)
WEST INDIA DOCKS
(Export)
Blackwall Basin
Cuckolds Point
CUBA STREET
South Dock
SURREY COMMERCIAL DOCKS (site of)
ISLE OF DOGS
MANCHESTER ROAD
River Thames
N
Limehouse Reach
HAVANNAH STREET
MARIA STREET
WEST
Inner
Millwall Docks
MILLWALL
FERRY ROAD
Outer
'Waterman's Arms' GLENGARNOCK AVE.
STEPNEY HIGH STREET
STEPNEY
CHAPEL HOUSE ST.
Island Gardens
River Thames
SCHOONER ST. (site of)
RATCLIFF
STREET
BARQUE ST. (site of)
Greenwich Reach
Royal Naval College
Cutty Sark
GREENWICH
NARROW ST.
Museum
Greenwich Park
Peter McClure 1990

Limehouse Days

also by Daniel Farson

JACK THE RIPPER
MARIE LLOYD AND MUSIC HALL
OUT OF STEP
THE MAN WHO WROTE DRACULA
IN PRAISE OF DOGS
A WINDOW ON THE SEA
HENRY: AN APPRECIATION OF HENRY WILLIAMSON
A TRAVELLER IN TURKEY
SOHO IN THE FIFTIES
SACRED MONSTERS
ESCAPADES
GALLERY

Fiction

THE DOG WHO KNEW TOO MUCH
SWANSDOWNE

LIMEHOUSE DAYS

A Personal Experience of the East End

Daniel Farson

MICHAEL JOSEPH LONDON

MICHAEL JOSEPH LTD
Published by the Penguin Group
27 Wrights Lane, London W8 5TZ, England
Viking Penguin Inc., 40 West 23rd Street, New York, New York 10010, USA
Penguin Books Australia Ltd, Ringwood, Victoria, Australia
Penguin Books Canada Ltd, 2801 John Street, Markham, Ontario, Canada L3R 1B4
Penguin Books (NZ) Ltd, 182–190 Wairau Road, Auckland 10, New Zealand

Penguin Books Ltd, Registered Offices: Harmondsworth, Middlesex, England

First published in Great Britain 1991

Typeset in Monophoto Photina 11/13pt
Typeset, printed and bound by Butler & Tanner Ltd, Frome, Somerset

A CIP catalogue record for this book is available from the British Library
ISBN 0 7181 3256 4

The quotations by Colin MacInnes on pages 169–70
are reproduced by permission of the Colin MacInnes Estate;
the quotations by W. Fishman from his *East End 1988* on pages 85–87
are reproduced by permission of Duckworth and Co. Ltd.

For Rose
of Broomfield Street E14

Contents

Acknowledgements

All photographs are by Daniel Farson, unless otherwise credited. The song-sheet covers are from the author's personal collection.

Inevitably, I have drawn on such classic sources as Mayhew's *London*; *London* by Gustave Doré and Blanchard Jerrold; *East London* by Walter Besant; *Limehouse Nights* by Thomas Burke; and *The People of the Abyss* by Jack London.

I am indebted also to: *The East Enders 1961* by Ashley Smith, and *This is Whitechapel* – a companion to the exhibition of photographs by Ian Berry at the Whitechapel Art Gallery 1972.

I have avoided reference to several recent books on the East End, for if I cover the same ground this would seem either redundant or plagiarist, and my aim is to relate my own personal experiences of the district after I moved to Limehouse and ran my pub on the Isle of Dogs.

However, I am indebted to Professor William Fishman for his study, *East End 1888* and the invaluable quotations he has gathered. If you wish to read a comprehensive study of the East End at that period, this can hardly be surpassed.

1

THE HOUSE ON THE BEND OF THE RIVER

THIS IS the story of my love affair with a place. Not simply with the house which leant over the river on the bend of the Thames at Limehouse, nor with Narrow Street behind, but with the East End as a whole and the people who lived there.

The history of the East End was short-lived. I had the good fortune to witness the last gasp of its vitality before the developers moved in, the people moved out and everything changed.

My discovery of the house on the river was not entirely due to luck, for I have always yearned to live beside water (and as I write this now I look out on the estuary of the Taw and Torridge rivers in North Devon). Working for television in the late 1950s, I stayed at my grandmother's elegant house in Pelham Place in South Kensington, but I needed a home of my home and I wanted it near to the Thames. The posher reaches beyond Chiswick were beyond me financially, and the *tête-à-tête* cluster of houseboats near Battersea Bridge did not appeal to me, for I found the *bonhomie* too forced. I was searching for somewhere unfashionable to the south of Tower Bridge where the working stretch of the river was darker, noisier, uglier, yet more alive.

It is one of the surprises of life that if you want something badly enough you can usually get it. But my search proved fruitless to begin with.

My first taste of this unfamiliar territory had been years before when I bicycled around the sites of the Jack the Ripper murders with Colin Wilson. When I worked for *Picture Post* as a photographer I was sent to the East End to cover the national mourning for the death of George VI, accompanied by the writer Maurice Richardson, a splendid *bon viveur* with the face and swagger of a former pugilist. Our journey proved all too abortive. Not only did my flash fail to work, but my camera was threatened by the few West Indians inside the shady pubs of Cable Street where Richardson had guided me: a far cry from the mass grief anticipated by my picture editor, who envisaged sentimental sing-songs and tears for the passing of the monarch, followed by a loyal cockney knees-up.

This was a typical misconception, as I discovered when I started to explore the territory in earnest one summer several years later. I set out on foot from Tower Bridge to Wapping and Shadwell, down the length of Ratcliff Highway and Cable Street. Restricted to weekends, I walked alone, meeting little traffic, finding that the East End had a curiously alien look, with the streets like dark, empty canyons, the tall warehouses shutting out the light, casting fierce black shadows, redeemed by patches of humanity as West Indian families sat on chairs outside their low-lying houses to catch the last of the evening sun.

Though it is hard to credit today when the East End seems so familiar and accessible, then it was a foreign territory, as if I had passed an invisible frontier post at Tower Bridge. When the American writer Jack London arrived to make his journey into the 'abyss' in 1902, he asked his smart West End friends exactly where the East End was situated, and they waved vaguely in an easterly direction. Little had changed. Few West Enders ventured East unless they were on business, or 'slumming' like the 'toffs' before them, who went to Ratcliff Highway escorted by a policeman who was well paid to protect them. Among his astounding engravings of London in the 1870s, Gustave Doré recorded a fight outside one of the 'dens' scattered along the highway, with the masts of the ships lining the river like a forest. An account referred to chairs and tables screwed to the floor to prevent them from being used as weapons. When there was a cry of 'Murder!', the policeman told his toffs: 'Stand still, gentlemen, this happens every five minutes in these parts.'

I was disappointed to find the East End considerably tamer, failing to realise in my naivety that it lay dormant in the daytime before bursting into life at night.

I took the river ferries to Greenwich, making notes of any places which looked habitable, returning afterwards on foot. I had no success. Most of the places proved derelict, and though I heard of a building which was owned by the river police and might be converted into flats in the future, I was not prepared to wait. It did not occur to me to consider restoring one of the crumbling houses at Shadwell Basin, for I did not have the slightest knowledge of mortgages or bank loans.

I gained the excitement of turning a corner and stumbling on a place I had not even noticed from the river – like the small pub the Town of Ramsgate at Wapping where the infamous Judge Jeffreys was caught while he was waiting for a ship to rescue him from his pursuers – but the general reaction to my enquiries confirmed that the Londoner was so indifferent to his river and its history that only a scattering of people lived beside it south of Tower Bridge, and then because they had to.

I was tempted to abandon my search; but then, in the way these things happen, I heard of a flat that was being converted in Narrow Street above a barge-repair yard at Limehouse. Simultaneously, Antony Armstrong-Jones told me that he had found a place on the river. I am still not certain if we were after the same house, but he changed his mind and in due course I was invited to his housewarming at the Little Midshipman at Rotherhithe on the other side of the Thames, since demolished after its final years of unexpected fame following his marriage to Princess Margaret.

Meanwhile, with a new spurt of determination, I tracked down the owners of the property in Narrow Street – the Woodward Fishers. Dolly (Dorathea) Fisher, sometimes referred to as 'the tugboat Annie of the Thames', commanded a fleet of 200 barges from the control room in her handsome house in Blackheath, cultivating a startling resemblance to George Arliss by wearing well-tailored suits, a stock, and sometimes a monocle. Everyone obeyed her, including her husband William, a born riverman. William was the winner of the coveted Doggett's Coat and Badge, the annual rowing race of six young watermen on 1 August, started in 1716 by an actor called Doggett to commemorate the accession of George I. As a prize he offered an orange coat of antique cut with a silver badge on the right sleeve denoting the White Horse of Hanover, hence the name, though this had been replaced by a gift of money. I grew to know the Woodward Fishers over the next few years, and though Mrs Fisher, who became my landlady, proved a splendidly vigorous octogenarian, one of the true characters of the old river, I never lost my fear of her.

Narrow Street

My house was above the lower sign which advertised Woodward Fisher.

My first meeting was with her son Ken, a courteous young man, smooth and citified in contrast to the rough background of his parents, who started their fleet with £20 and a single barge, subsequently absorbing the wharf owned by W.N. Sparks and Sons, builder of wooden sailing barges. I doubt if I had been inside the house at this stage, yet I was in love with the idea of it and so desperate that I made the misplaced gesture of inviting Ken Fisher to lunch at Wheeler's in the hope of impressing him, bringing my secretary from Television House as bait: she had a remarkable resemblance to Marilyn Monroe.

Nonplussed, he did his utmost to dissuade me, stressing that the place was unsuitable except for a hardened East Ender or impoverished students. This was followed by my first meeting with Dolly Fisher in Narrow Street, where she led me to the balcony and pointed out the disadvantages with scrupulous honesty: the excruciating scream of the electric scrapers as they removed the rust from the worn-out barges; the grime from the coal-loading wharf near by, settling a layer of black dust where we stood; the smell, or rather the stink of the river at low tide.

But I could hear no noise, see no dirt, smell no smell. This was what I had yearned for; the reality surpassed the dream. I saw the two wild duck making their nest in the pilings of the coal-wharf, and a flight of swans beating their way down the river in single file. I relished the sight of a barge being rowed upstream with the tide, the men with their long poles standing out in silhouette against the shimmering Thames.

Beneath her gruff exterior, with that bark of a voice frequently mistaken for a man's as she roused her workmen from their tea-breaks on the radio, Dolly Fisher was a kind if abrasive woman, and she sensed my passion – and indeed she shared my romance with the river. Laughing at my anxiety, she mentioned a figure for the rent and became my new landlady.

Why did I love Narrow Street so much? It was only natural: I had found the place I was looking for. I was so enthusiastic that I moved in before the arrival of the furniture, sleeping on a mattress on the floor. Mrs Fisher intended to leave the proverbial 'loaf of bread, lump of coal, and a cellar of salt, just to bring you luck' but forgot the wine and confused the date.

Other reactions were less cordial and found my enthusiasm bewildering. A friend asked how I could sleep at night while the barges thundered together at high tide in the wake of passing ships. I countered that this was preferable to the din of traffic, and compared the trumpeting of the sirens of the cargo ships as they waited to enter Regent's Canal Dock to great animals approaching a waterhole in the jungle. He snorted at such romantic tosh and reminded me of the rat, apparently a large one, which lived in the attic, and the fumes which rose so violently from the barge-yard below that they lifted the carpet. Even I felt a sense of infinite relief when the yard closed for the night and the workmen departed, leaving a sense of peace – but my enthusiasm was unquenched.

My mother gazed around her sadly; worst of all, my devoted grandmother made the journey to Limehouse and gave the place her blessing, but suffered a stroke on the day I moved from Pelham Place, as if my departure was the cause. Guilt made me less considerate to her than I should have been. Also, I was too preoccupied, devouring every scrap of history I could glean, visiting the archives of the Port of London Authority and reading books; and I bought an engraving by Whistler which showed the barge-yard in 1854, surprisingly unchanged except that then the work was done by hand.

I acquired old prints which confirmed the age of my small Elizabethan house with the original brick and timber. An engraving of *A View taken near Limehouse Bridge, looking down the Thames* in 1751 showed the Dutch-style roof, twinned with the house next door, and a covered balcony clearly marked 'Wine', with Limehouse Cut beside it. Like so many waterfront houses on the Thames, mine had been a small pub called the Waterman's Arms, and I found a print of the small room which was now my sitting-room, with a couple of benches, a bare table and a big fire. Sailors and East Enders sheltered from the cold, and the beer was 2*d.* a pint and no doubt twice as strong.

The river outside was in a constant state of flux and never failed to fascinate: on one side I could see the famous pub the Prospect of Whitby and the towers of Tower Bridge looming in the far distance; to the other, after Limehouse Reach, the river swept round a five-mile curve to Greenwich. Opposite was a desolate stretch known as Cuckold's Point, backed by a few factory chimneys.

There were 5,000 barges on the Thames in the late fifties and tugs led strings of them past me in a constant parade joined by dirty freighters, with trees tied to their masts on Christmas Day, and ships with names like *Velazquez* or the *Cyprian Shore*, with smaller coasters from France which were family boats with lines of laundry and dogs scampering along the decks.

Sometimes something special: a liner from Poland with the passengers staring as they passed; naval frigates, even a submarine; the *Britannia* with Princess Margaret and Lord Snowdon (as Armstrong-Jones had now become) waving to a group of us as they sailed on their wedding day for the West Indies; hovercraft; motor boats and racing skiffs; yachts; and old barges with rust-coloured sails. The Thames was still alive with all the flotsam and jetsam of maritime life, arriving and leaving for destinations I could only imagine. Several years earlier I had sailed around the world in the Merchant Navy and now I felt linked to the sea again. Dolly Fisher understood: 'I am so glad you love the river,' she wrote to me. 'I do, and I love the sea equally well. To my mind no scenery is perfect without water, be it only a wee pond.'

I began to learn the lore of the Thames, and its eccentricities. There was no speed limit and no particular side of the river to keep to, but if a boatman

fished up a corpse on the south side he received a reward of 7*s*. 6*d*., but only 6*s*. on the north. Not surprisingly, the bodies were delivered to the south. The river police, three men in a boat on eight-hour shifts, picked up an average of seventy dead bodies and forty live ones a year. The gravel beach exposed below me at low tide was a well-known resting place, and sure enough the body of an old woman was discovered there a few days after I moved in.

It was here that Charles Dickens set the opening for *Our Mutual Friend*, with Rogue Riderhood patrolling the river for floating corpses which he could rob, or claim the reward. 'It's a curious thing,' wrote Dickens, 'but the river sweeps in here and the tide settles the bodies among the piles and craft. Rogue knew that.'

A view taken near Limehouse Bridge, looking down the Thames

It was claimed that Dickens stayed at Number 92, and the bow-windowed pub the Bunch of Grapes, a few houses to the right of me, sported a Dickens Room because the Six Jolly Fellowship Porters in the book was allegedly based on it. To my delight, and the considerable annoyance of the landlord, I discovered an old print of the Two Brewers to the other side of me at Limehouse Cut which was closer to Dickens' description of a 'tavern of dropsical appearance . . . with a crazy wooden verandah impending over the water; indeed the whole house, inclusive of the complaining flag-staff on the roof, impended over the water, but seemed to have got into the condition of a faint-hearted diver who has paused so long on the brink that he will never go in at all.' Plainly, this was the original for the Fellowship Porters instead of the neatly fronted Grapes, but the Brewers had long since gone and it was tactless to make the correction with so much glee. The Grapes sports the Dickens association today and why not? He may well have drunk there too.

An early faded print of the Two Brewers

I explored the maze of streets inland with such evocative names as Gin Alley, Cinnamon Street, Ropemakers Fields and Kidney Stairs; and learnt that Narrow Street used to be Fore Street and Limehouse Street before that, probably taking the name from the lime kilns at the end which dated back to the fourteenth century. Duke Shore Stairs, the cut beside me where the Brewers used to hang so dropsically, had been known as Dick Shore or Shoar, apparently a corruption of Sewer.

Searching for decorations for my rooms in Narrow Street, I found a crowded junk shop in Cable Street run by a coloured man with tribal slashes on his cheeks, and bought a jaunty earthenware figure of what appeared to be a cloth-capped newsboy, except that the Extra Special placard he was holding advertised: 'Greenlees CLAYMORE The Favourite Scotch Everywhere.' It cost a few shillings and continues to give me pleasure. I was interested to find a postcard in the Victoria and Albert Museum recently of a similar figure dated 1910.

I found equally useless objects in Bermondsey Market on Saturday mornings, but was unimaginative in buying my furniture from Heal's, helped by an advance on my salary from Associated-Rediffusion. The floorboards were blasted; black-and-white vinyl tiles lined a room that led to the balcony; and I indulged myself with the extravagance of a patterned block of Italian marble from an antique shop in Pimlico, which was mounted in a brass base to provide a table. This formed the focal point of my sitting-room, which was so small that I expanded it visually with a mirror, from the junk shop in Cable Street, which stretched from the floor to the ceiling. My pictures ranged from a couple of large ship portraits, painted by a member of the crew, which I bought for 30*s*. each from a shop near Holborn, to a large black-and-white head by Frank Auerbach which faced my bed; I studied it each morning wondering if the figure was Christ, Abraham Lincoln, or the person, apparently a lady, whom he has painted so often using the initials J.Y.M. This remains my favourite of all his work. Other paintings included Lucian Freud's portrait of John Deakin, and two generous gifts: a study of Somerset Maugham given to me by Graham Sutherland, and the head of a surgeon retrieved from Francis Bacon before he could destroy it. On my grandmother's death I inherited a drawing of a tiger by Gaudier-Brzeska, dazzling in the simplicity of just a few lines. I also made the satisfying rediscovery of old possessions, odds and ends accumulated over the years.

The Victorian black iron fireplaces still existed: one had a double curve of unusual elegance, but the one in my sitting-room had been removed and modernised. I tried to redeem it with an expensive wooden frame.

There was no ground floor, but stairs to the sitting-room which had once been the pub, and two smaller rooms leading to the river. The kitchen and bathroom were moved towards the street, unlike the old days when the river was considered so foul that the street was regarded as more respectable. Two larger rooms upstairs, with my bedroom facing the river and the other spare; and a useful attic with a smaller bedroom to which I sometimes retreated, for it was quieter, with a welcome sense of isolation.

I created a substitute garden in the tiny yard which led to the balcony, with bay trees in tubs, and plants and creepers in empty barrels and window-boxes, and when the weather was good I ate my meals and typed outside.

Dolly Fisher approved. Writing to me on 9 June 1958, she concluded: 'We are all delighted with all you have done. I am very glad that I personally took the flat in hand and had the bathroom and kitchen fitted. Can you imagine that the kitchen was where your study is and the "wash-house", with all that name implies, was where your "fernery" is now, and the "parlour", and it was a parlour, overlooked Narrow Street? Carry on your good work.'

Within a month, I had settled in, with the advantage of the summer ahead of me. Because I appeared on television, my arrival had been noticed and I was startled when pleasure boats announced it as they coasted by, culminating with the loudspeaker of the crowded steamer which swept past soon after nine on Sunday morning – and I could tell the time by it – on its way to Gravesend: 'This is Limehouse – once notorious for vice and opium dens and now the home of TV personality Daniel Farson.' This left me pleased, though slightly shaken. If someone had crashed out on the sofa after a Saturday night party and was woken by the announcement, they were dumbfounded.

Gradually, the East Enders realised that my affection for the district was not affected and they accepted me, though they could not understand why I liked it so much when it was their ambition to move out. Even so, they were pleased and slightly flattered. I became an 'honorary East Ender'.

I exchanged my former neighbour in Pelham Place, Cecil Beaton, with a retired punch-drunk boxer called Chalky who lived in the upper flat next door. I made countless friends, and came to understand the unique qualities of the people who lived there. The East Ender was so tough that he could afford to be sentimental, even chivalrous. There was a gallantry which you could not find anywhere else in the south of England. There was the strongest sense of family that I have come across.

2

THE SHOCKING HISTORY, AND CONRAD'S MISTAKE AT THE EASTERN HOTEL

STUDYING THE history of the East End, I was surprised by its brevity. While the heart of London festered like a great wen as 'The Metropolis of the Empire', the outskirts were isolated. Two hundred years earlier, the Hackney Marshes were literally that, marshland covered at every tide, while the Isle of Dogs was unpopulated apart from a Chapel House, a dairy and a farm noted for its grazing.

Further inland, there were open fields, orchards and acres of waving corn. A Bishop's Palace acted as a church for the parish of Stebenhithe (from the Saxon chieftain Stebba) which became Stepney, and though the land belonged to the bishop the populace of London had the right to hunt there, for the marshes teemed with wild birds.

'Wheresoever you look,' wrote Sir Thomas More in 1504, 'the earth yieldeth you a pleasant prospect; the temperature of the air fresheth you, and the very bounds of the heavens do delight you. Here you find nothing but bounteous gifts of nature and saint-like tokens of innocency.'

When a sea wall rejected the tides, reclaiming land from the river, mills started to line the Isle of Dogs, and villages like Hackney and Bow were added to those which already stood on higher and healthier ground beside the river, such as Ratcliff (or Ratcliffe), named after the red cliff above the shore where Frobisher set sail 'for the search of the passage to China', and Limehouse, which Raleigh left on his third voyage to Guyana.

Today's anachronistic label of the Tower Hamlets was accurate at the end of the last century, when it embraced Whitechapel, Stepney, Wapping, Limehouse, Poplar, Mile End Old and New, Bow and Bromley, the federation of the East End bordered by the River Lea to the east, the Thames to the south, Hackney and Shoreditch to the north, and the City of London to the West End.

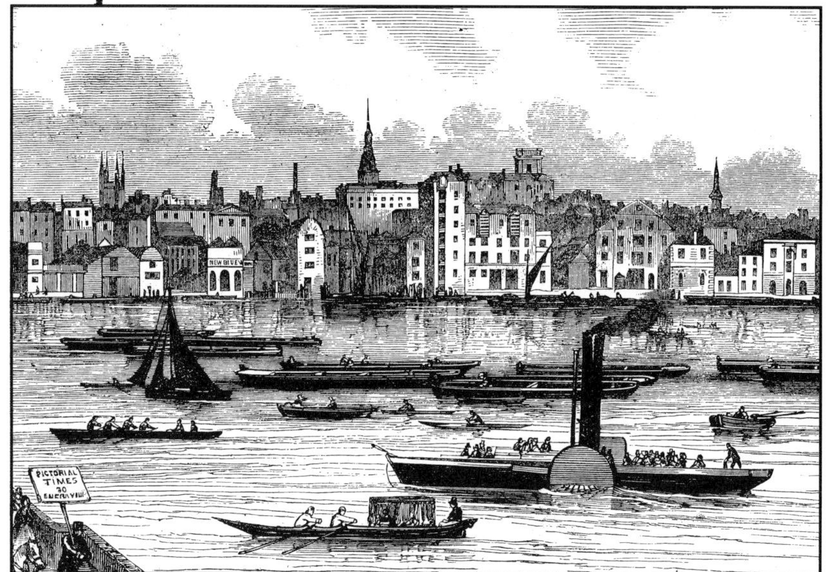

An example of river traffic at St Martin's and Ludgate Hill

By then, the character of the district had been transformed. Gradually the villages had outgrown themselves as they joined together, losing their particular identities. The greatest upheaval was caused by the discovery of the Indies as their wealth poured into East India and West India Docks, continuing into London on swaying trucks down East India Dock, West India Dock and Commercial Roads; but the wealth failed to enrich, changing it completely for the worse. The degradation was described dramatically by J.H. Mackay in *The Anarchists* (1891): 'The East End of London is the hell of poverty. Like the enormous black, motionless, giant Kraken, the poverty of London lies there in lurking silence and encircles with its mighty tentacles the life and wealth of the City and of the West End' – except that its tentacles did not have the strength to reach the City, let alone embrace its wealth. The term 'East Ender' had become a description of someone unfortunate, to be pitied or ignored.

We cannot conceive of the nineteenth-century conditions today. We blur the boundaries, forgetting that the Port of London was as strange as Port Said to those staid Victorians in the safety of their West End homes with their servants tucked securely below stairs. We speak of the 'quality of life', but such a phrase would have been meaningless to those whose future offered no hope but a greater wretchedness as they grew older and the women lost their looks and usefulness. Women suffered most, because they were weaker from being kept indoors, since many were occupied making matchboxes at home, where the fumes could be lethal, mingling with those rising from the cellars which were used as open cesspits.

The East End had also been the shock absorber for the new population of migrants. The Huguenots, who escaped from France after the revocation of the Edict of Nantes in 1685, brought their Calvinist beliefs and silk-manufacturing skills, enhancing the area at Spitalfields, where they settled in the elegant houses of Fournier Street with a barrier at the end to protect them from the *hoi polloi*. They were few in numbers and presented no problem, but they were followed by the Irish in the eighteenth century and then by Russian and Polish Jews, who settled in Whitechapel in their thousands in the last century, estimated at 100,000 altogether. Unable to speak the language of their new country, they kept to themselves, speaking in their native tongues. Even when I arrived, and visited the Grand Palais Yiddish Theatre in Commercial Road, I met old men in the Zekeinim Club afterwards who had never learnt English.

The great Port of London, founded at the beginning of the nineteenth century had made the East End a melting pot of nationalities, with the Chinese at Limehouse and Lascars from West India Docks near by, and other foreign sailors hurrying ashore in search of drink and women, rich from their months at sea. Many would be robbed and rolled before the night was over.

Half-noticed in the shadows were the destitute nomads, the raddled prostitutes who had known younger days though they were far from old, and the pickpockets who darted through the jostling crowds. White-faced children were pushed aside as they proffered their pathetic wares of two or three onions or a turnip, scarcely noticed in the swarm. The markets of Commercial Road had the romance of oriental bazaars, but the sidestreets ran with refuse in the gutters, while the despised midden-men in the lowest profession of all ran with buckets of human excrement to empty in the sewers. Passers-by clutched their scarves to their nostrils to reduce the poisonous fumes from the dust-heaps and cesspits below the rickety houses which practically leant against each other, anxious to dodge the chamber-pots emptied from the windows above.

Constant noise added to the inferno, with the screams of animals driven towards the abattoirs in sidestreets which were stained with their blood. Margaret Harkness, who wrote *In Darkest London: Captain Lobo, Salvation Army* in 1889 under the pseudonym of John Law, described a herd of frightened sheep being driven over the sawdust: 'Their bleating was piteous! At their feet ran a dog barking. Men in blue coats drove them along with sticks, callous of their terror and distress. Many people in the East End enjoyed these sights. Some will climb up walls to see a bullock stunned with a pike, or a calf's throat cut.' Sadly that has always been the stuff of the slaughter-house, and she noticed a universal cruelty: 'The scum is brutal, the refined are vicious'. The American Mackay was particularly shocked by children 'amusing themselves by the sight of the dying fits of a cat whose eyes they had gouged out, and whom they had hanged by the tail. When the bleeding, tortured animal jerked with his feet to get away, they struck at it with the cruel awful pleasure children take in visible pain.'

Another view of the Two Brewers

The East End had exploded: London's population, it was rumoured, surpassed a staggering total of a million people and was growing all the time. Thousands roamed the streets at night, crashing down wherever they could, huddled together for warmth, turning to opium, and laudanum which contained it, for release. And unlike the sad young vagrants of today, they had no alternative.

With such congestion, even those who were able to live indoors were devoid of privacy or space. In 1883, Andrew Mearns described in *The Bitter Cry of Outcast London*, how at least one and often two families would live in a single room, and sometimes a lodger as well. In the cellar of one tenement, a sanitary inspector found a couple with their three children and four pigs, while a missionary saw a man dying from smallpox, his wife recovering from her eighth confinement, and the children running about half-naked; another room was shared by seven people and 'a little dead child'.

Wretched physical conditions might be bearable when there is hope, but there was little of that. The main concern was to stay alive. Mearns encountered a family busily making matchboxes and parodies of furs, and he choked from the air which was 'laden with the particles of the superfluous fur pulled from the skins of rabbits, rats, dogs and other animals in preparation for the furrier. Here the smell of paste and of drying matchboxes, mingling with other sickly odours, overpowers you.' At least they had some means for survival, but the use of sweated labour for manufacturing matches was so brutal that the human spirit could not endure it, culminating triumphantly with the matchgirls' strike in 1888 at Bryant and May when 800 girls defied their employer and formed the Union of Women Match Makers.

Many people shared a bed, sleeping in shifts of eight hours each; yet this was preferable to the humiliation of the Casual Hostels where shame was the punishment for their misfortune. Those who accepted charity were stripped naked for a communal bath and thrust into a tiny cell, eight feet by four, with no furniture. Breaking stones, pounding them into dust which was sieved through a grille in the wall, was made compulsory in order to earn their keep. Half a ton of stones had to be pounded or four pounds of oakum picked in return for gruel and bread that scarcely filled a teacup. When Jack London stayed a night in such a hostel, he was horrified to see the back of a man: 'A mass of blood from attacks of vermin and retaliatory scratching.' At midnight he woke to find a rat on his chest.

An early photograph in *Streets of London* by William Shipman shows men in a Salvation Army hostel sleeping side by side in long beds that look like fish boxes and probably were. General William Booth opened a lodging house in 1888, the year of the murderer Jack the Ripper, charging 3*d.* a night with soup at ½*d.* for adults and a farthing for children, with compulsory prayer as the penalty for poverty. Nothing was free. One of the Ripper's victims was walking the streets because she had been turned away from a hostel for the lack of a few pence. Understandably, she had turned to prostitution. If death was the ultimate release, there was the slight satisfaction of delaying it if you sold your body.

Escape! Girls must have dreamt of it, especially if they lived in one of those houses where thirty people slept on straw in a single room where screams would be greeted with laughter if a girl was assaulted. Youth was short-lived in such conditions. A group of girls applying for work at a factory in 1889 were described as having faces 'wise with wickedness and eyes out of which all traces of maidenhood had vanished'. If they were lucky they earned 5*d.* a day; even so they managed to be generous among themselves, especially on the occasion of death, when the corpse was granted a decent departure without the stigma of the pauper's grave.

I am prejudiced against the Salvation Army: when I moved into Narrow Street I offered a bottle of beer to every old man at the nearby Salvation Army hostel after someone told me this was the one thing they missed with their Christmas lunch. My suggestion was refused indignantly, and I could not help noticing the hypocrisy as uniformed members of the 'Sally Army' toured the local pubs with their over-bright smiles and collecting boxes yet preached the evils of drink. I noticed that the hardened drinkers in the pub gave generously, apart from myself.

Yet General Booth showed perspicacity, if not great compassion, in his attitude towards the 'unfortunates', remarking that 'a young, penniless girl, if she be pretty, is often hunted from pillar to post by her employers, confronted always by the alternatives – Starve or Sin.' He observed that 'the profession of a prostitute is the only career in which the maximum income is paid to the newest apprentice', and looks could fade quickly so close to the waterfront where a virulent form of syphilis was carried by the Lascars and Malays, with no penicillin to prevent it. Booth described a typical prostitute as 'grimy and unwashed, her hands so black and filthy that mustard-and-cress might have been sown on them. An animated bundle of rags.' Yet how could she have been otherwise?

Walter Besant, one of the observers who were most concerned, saw boys and girls who found another form of release in drink: 'The girls, poor creatures, worse than the boys. I spoke to one. She was no more than thirteen or so – a pretty child, but helplessly intoxicated. When I spoke to her she tried to reply, but became inarticulate; she gasped, she laughed – the awful laugh of a drunkard! She made a gesture of helplessness, she fell sideways on the pavement, and would not rise. Her companions, as far gone as herself, only laughed. A sad sight, truly, in a civilised country.'

That was the indictment.

Black Lion Wharf *by James McNeill Whistler*

Yet it was not the whole truth.

After moving into Narrow Street I often walked to West India Dock Road and at the end of it paused for a drink in the Eastern Hotel at the junction with East India Dock Road which joined Commercial Road opposite Limehouse Church, designed by Hawksmoor.

Limehouse church designed by Nicholas Hawksmoor (1661–1736), a pupil of Wren

The Eastern was wooden and old-fashioned, and it pleased me to imagine it when it really was a hotel, one of the few in the East End. I came across a reference to it in Joseph Conrad's *Chance*, and realised that this was the place where one of his captains stayed after he docked near by.

Conrad described the scene outside with 'vans swaying like mountains' laden with riches, contrasting cruelly with

> the inhabitants of that end of the town where life goes on unadorned by grace or splendour; they passed us in their shabby garments, with sallow faces, haggard, anxious or weary, or simply without expression, in an unsmiling sombre stream not made up of lives but of mere unconsidered existences whose joys, struggles, thoughts, sorrows and their very hopes were miserable, glamourless, and of no account in the world.

I have seen such people myself. I photographed such a man in Brick Lane, a 'shabby genteel' with stained bowler hat and frayed collar, who had made this poignant effort yet passed me without expression in his eyes except for the recognition that his life was nearly over. Such people must have been legion when Conrad's captain stayed at the Eastern Hotel.

This photograph has haunted me ever since I took it. It shows quite clearly a man who has come face to face with death

Yet I believe that in spite of his genius, Conrad was wrong. Perhaps his Polish nationality had something to do with this, also his lengthy absences at sea, but I dare to suggest that he understood the East better than the East End.

Conrad failed to see that there had to be grace and glamour in such surroundings. The East Enders had to defy them or go under, and they did so with the gaiety of cockney wit and rhyming slang, and, above all, in Music Hall.

When Marie Lloyd, who was born and bred in the East End, staggered on stage clutching her old cock linnet in its little wooden cage, she confided to the audience that she had to move away:

> 'Cos the rent we couldn't pay,
> The moving van came round just after dark;
> There was me and my old man
> Shoving things inside the van,
> Which we'd often done before, let me remark.

The audience roared. Booze and bailiffs and moonlight flits – they *knew*. And later on the bill, Marie might appear in her Directoire Dress – 'quite a fashion-plate' – and it heartened them that one of their own could look so glamorous. This was the strength of the East Enders: that against the odds they could laugh at adversity, and having laughed, the adversity was less appalling.

'Unadorned by grace'? The grace of life in the East End was miraculous.

3

The Lowest Penny Gaff, and the Highest Aspirations for Culture

MUSIC HALL was a genuine example of a people's entertainment, created by them and for them. Though it was born on the posher side of the Thames in the Canterbury Hall at Lambeth, its rightful home was the East End, where it enhanced life. Due to the general illiteracy and the melting-pot of nationalities, there had been a craving for entertainment since the start of the last century, and it took various forms.

One of the antecedents to Music Hall, and the lowest form of entertainment, were the Penny Gaffs. Providing a distraction for the poorest inhabitants of the East End who could afford only a penny, the earlier Penny Gaffs were dense and dark, and were held in a converted shop or stable. Garish pictures outside enticed the passers-by and the show began when enough people had paid their pennies to go in, rather like the boxing booths of a fairground today. Reserved seats cost *2d.*, and the Gaff closed at midnight, after as many as six performances.

It was a rough and ready mixture of comedy, tragedy, singing, dancing and farce. The stage consisted of a few boards, with several musicians – often German – perched on a nearby table playing the fiddle, cornet, fife and flute. As many as 200 people sat on benches and when they were pleased they threw extra pennies on stage to supplement the performers' nightly wages of 10*d.* Roughly painted canvas served as the scenery and the whole affair was lit by candles.

The audience was young, usually from eight to twenty, mostly girls. Failing to recognise the East End genius in ferreting out humour in the midst of squalor, and to suspect young people who were having fun, the Establishment accused the Gaffs of being a training ground for thieves and pickpockets. 'I have no doubt that a very large majority of those who afterwards find their way to the bar of the Old Bailey may trace their career in crime to their attendance at a Penny Theatre,' James Grant declared pompously in 1830. The Gaffs dismayed such a hardened observer as Blanchard Jerrold, who explored London for his book with Gustave Doré and knew the worst excesses that the East End indulged in. He found 'jollity' in the dens of Ratcliff, but none here:

> The true Penny Gaff is the place where juvenile poverty meets juvenile crime. We elbowed our way into one that was the foulest, dingiest place of entertainment I can conceive ... The narrow passages were blocked by sharp-eyed young thieves, who could tell the policeman at a glance, through the thin disguise of private clothes ...
>
> 'This does more harm than anything I know of,' said the sergeant, as he pointed to the pack of girls and boys who were laughing, talking, gesticulating, hanging over the boxes – and joining in the chorus of a song the trio were singing.
>
> An overwhelming cocked hat, a prodigious shirt collar, straps reaching half-way to the knees, grotesque imitations of that general enemy known to the Whitechapel loafer as a 'swell', caricatures of the police ...

Possibly this is why Jerrold and his sergeant took such offence, for they would have been recognised as the 'swell' and his police escort, and they were 'slumming', conspicuous in their condescension.

Jerrold wrote with startling squeamishness: 'The odour – the atmosphere to begin with, is indescribable. The rows of brazen young faces are terrible to look upon. It is impossible to be angry with their sauciness, or to resent the leers and grimaces that are directed upon us as unwelcome intruders.' At least he appreciated that, but he concluded with a melodramatic flourish: 'Some have the aspect of wild cats. The lynx at bay has not a crueller glance than some I caught from almost baby faces.'

Even Henry Mayhew, the most impartial of observers, was shocked by the entertainment he witnessed. This featured a fourteen-year-old who danced with 'more energy than grace' and a comic in a battered hat who sang a song, 'the whole point of which consisted in the mere utterance of some filthy word at the end of each stanza.' Mayhew conceded: 'Nothing could have been more successful.' Another song called 'Pine-apple rock', with a rhyme that can be imagined, produced tears of 'enjoyment of the poison ... it was absolutely awful to behold the relish with which the young ones jumped to the hideous meaning of the verses.' Yet, as Marie Junior told me of her mother's notorious songs, 'they would seem like bleedin' hymns today.'

The Gaff he visited even sported a drag act – 'perfect in its wickedness' – which Mayhew took very seriously.

> A ballet began between a man dressed as a woman, and a country clown. The most disgusting attitudes were struck, the most immoral acts

> represented, without one dissenting voice. If there had been any feat of agility, any grimacing, or in fact, anything with which the laughter of the uneducated classes is usually associated, the applause might have been accounted for; but here were two ruffians degrading themselves each time they stirred a limb, and forcing into the brains of the childish audience before them thoughts that must embitter a lifetime, and descend from father to child like some bodily infirmity.

That last remark had an uneasy relevance, for it was one of the unpleasant characteristics of the Gaff that cripples were exhibited as an attraction, like the freaks in the old raree-shows, transported in boxes to be exhibited at Bartholomew's Fair near Smithfield. This dated back to 1685, when a father wrote to his son of 'Others born in any monstrous shape, or having children as such, here celebrate their misery, and, by getting money, forget how odious they are made.' When Charles Dickens visited the Greenwich Fair in 1835 he referred to the dwarfs as 'objects of great curiosity', mentioning a living skeleton, a wild Indian and a beautiful young lady with white hair and pink eyes – plainly an albino; also, the celebrated 'pig-faced woman'. But it was the dwarf who attracted the writer most, living in a box two feet six inches high painted like a house. Once inside he fired a pistol from the first-floor window. Dickens remarked that it was hardly surprising that the 'unfortunate little object was always particularly drunk.'

In the East End the Penny Gaffs were famous for such oddities as a mermaid, and an unfortunate dog 'with lion's claws' whose paws had been split. In a Gaff in the Mile End Road, a little girl turned the handle of an organ until a man without arms appeared who could shave himself, play a violin and perform numerous feats with his toes, billed as 'A credit to his Maker'.

The armless cripple was fortunate compared to another exhibit discovered by Dr Frederick Treves in an empty greengrocer's shop in Whitechapel Road in 1884, which had a life-sized portrait hanging outside, advertising the price of admission as *2d*. 'This very crude production,' wrote Treves, 'depicted a frightful creature that could only have been possible in a nightmare. The fact that it was still human was the most repellent attribute of the creature. There was nothing about it of the pitiableness of the misshapen or deformed, nothing of the grotesqueness of the freak, but merely the loathsome insinuation of a man being changed into an animal.' Treves was taken inside:

> The showman – speaking as if to a dog – called out harshly 'Stand up!' The thing arose slowly and let the blanket that covered its head and back fall to the ground. There stood revealed the most disgusting specimen of humanity that I have ever seen ... at no time had I met with such a degraded or perverted specimen of a human being. He was naked to the waist, his feet bare, he wore a pair of threadbare trousers that once belonged to some fat gentleman's dress suit.

For Joseph Merrick, who suffered so severely from the elephantiasis which exposed him to public stares and ridicule, the doctor's visit proved his salvation. Recognising the man who lurked behind the animal, Treves returned to save him from his wretchedness, caring for him in the London Hospital near by where he gained a certain dignity and even fame, taken up by the aristocracy and visited by Princess Alexandra. However, it can be argued that the much maligned showman of the Gaff, Tom Norman, also saved Merrick, for without his protection – even his exhibition as a freak – what would have become of the Elephant Man?

The Committee of the Whitechapel Board of Works objected to the Gaffs as 'public nuisances' and 'a serious injury' to the local tradesmen, apart from being an 'annoyance to the respectable inhabitants of the district'. They had a case, but their attempts to close the Gaffs failed, for they underestimated the resilient role which the Gaffs performed in the East End, as did the later, grander Music Halls.

The Gaffs also poked fun at everyday calamities, and so reduced them. Another squeamish observer, the journalist Augustus Sala, complained that the entertainment was 'so real': 'The audience are delighted. Mr S reproaches Mrs S with the possession of a private gin bottle' (a forerunner of Marie's old girl who had been 'knocked abaht a bit' by the Cromwell Arms); 'Mrs S inveighs against the hideous turpitude of Mr S for pawning three pillow-cases to purchase beer. The audiences are in ecstasies. A sturdy coal-heaver in the stalls slaps his thighs with delight. Ugh! terribly real.'

Surely Sala and the other reformers were naive in failing to appreciate that the 'ecstasies' of the audience were due to recognition, and there seems little harm in that. Gradually, however, the Gaffs improved. When George Sims paid 3*d.* for a seat in a private box at The Garrick in Leman Street, it was such a grand Gaff that it began to be referred to as a Music Hall. He witnessed a moment of East End gallantry:

> Two negroes, a sailor and a lady were the other occupants and they supped during the performance. Their supper, which consisted of trotters, was thrown up to them by a man in the pit who walked about and shouted his dainties. At the end of the play there was one trotter not eaten and this the sailor, carried away by his feelings, threw at the virtuous heroine as she spoke the tag. She picked it up, bowed her thanks to our box and carried it off with as much grace as a leading lady at the West End would have carried off a bouquet.

On another occasion, the audience barracked a refined lady vocalist so cruelly, with catcalls and whistles, that someone shouted out – 'Give the poor old cow a chance, can't you!'

'Thank God,' she called back. 'At least there is *one* gentleman in the house.'

The Penny Gaffs illustrate the craving for culture in the East End and a need for theatre from which the Music Halls were to be born.

Until the Theatres Act of 1843, theatres were not allowed to present plays. They were prevented from doing so by Royal Charters, enjoyed by Drury Lane and Covent Garden, and by a Licensing Act dating back to 1737, which established the Lord Chamberlain as censor. It was a role he fulfilled until the second half of this century; and the Act decreed that anyone who worked for gain without a licence from the King was 'deemed a rogue and a vagabond'.

The New Royal Pavilion Theatre, Whitechapel Road

This helps to explain the ill-repute of actors. In 1787, an actor called John Palmer fought the Act when he opened the Royalty Theatre in Wellclose

Square. The official Royal Theatres retaliated with an advertisement which stressed the penalties involved and scared off some of his fellow actors, while the Society for the Suppression of Vice protested against the 'revival of scenic exhibitions', even though the Royalty was an elegant building holding 2,500 people and the play was a benefit performance of *As You Like It.* Although the Royalty was in one of the roughest parts of the East End, the surrounding streets were choked with carriages by four o'clock on the day of the opening.

With considerable courage, Palmer addressed the audience: 'tumblers and dancing dogs might appear unmolested before you, but other performers and myself standing forward to exhibit a moral play is deemed a crime.'

Sure enough, Palmer was arrested under the Act as a rogue, vagabond or sturdy beggar. He met the magistrate in a public house and was so certain that he was going to be sent to prison that he asked if he could fetch certain documents in his defence. After a long wait, the magistrate realised he had been locked inside, but Palmer was caught and though released on bail he found the opposition too overwhelming, and gave up the battle.

A middle-class God exacerbated the church's hostility to the theatre. Over half the theatres of the East End were burnt until fire regulations were enforced of such strictness that the smallest could not afford to keep them and went out of business. (Later, around 200 Music Halls were closed, unable to meet the Certificate of Suitability Law in 1878.)

The Royalty was burnt down in 1826, and rebuilt as the Brunswick, which enjoyed one of the briefest lives in theatrical history. The façade was magnificent, with walls 118 feet high; ill-advisedly, they were only two and a half bricks wide. Two days after the opening, bits began to fall from the heavy roof made of iron until the entire theatre buckled and collapsed, killing fifteen people. Inevitably, the unctuous local clergyman saw this as an act of retribution against theatres in general. Instead of a memorial, he gave an indictment: 'Of late years the theatre that stood there was a most convenient focus of all the depravity of the most fearful neighbourhood in London.' Continuing in the florid tradition of the pulpit, he referred to the enormity of crime

> too vast not to make men tremble lest the wrath of God should visit the people in some general and awful manner. All this depravity was most fatally assisted by the late theatre. Indeed, it was a grand centre of abandoned publicans, Jews, crimps, brothel keepers, thieves and harlots with all the lowest and vilest who lived upon the plunder of sailors ... The theatre necessarily and essentially draws around it all that is vile and guilty ... where the carcase is, there the eagles will be gathered together to feed on and destroy their prey.

So much for Christian tolerance.

Because of the Licensing Act, the 'minor' theatres in the East End could only present plays in the guise of charity benefits or musicals. If they resorted to the subterfuge of a 'burletta' with songs and music, even their beloved Shakespeare could be staged, which led to the absurdity of a production of *Othello* with a musician playing a chord on the piano every five minutes, so softly that it did not distract from the play. One Penny Gaff which dared to stage *Othello* straight was raided by the police and the cast and the audience were taken to the station where they were fined the next morning.

Due to this absurdity, the small East End theatres were forced to present Variety, with the irony that the Royal Theatres were so unsuccessful with straight drama that in order to keep their audiences they had to plunder their lesser rivals in the East End for the acts they despised: such as the Human Fly, a man who crawled over the ceiling of Drury Lane by means of suction, and performing lions.

This was the height – or should it be the depth – of irony: that the East End theatres were condemned as a bad influence and a meeting-place for thieves, but their craving for culture was ignored. Far from wishing to present filth, they asked for the right to stage Shakespeare.

In spite of busybody committees attempting to impede it, the campaign against the licensing laws gained strength. Bulwar Lytton supported one of the first resolutions to abolish the law in Parliament in 1832, attacking the monopoly 'which condemns the masterpieces of Shakespeare, whose very nature seems to scorn all petty bounds, fetters and limitations, to be performed at only two theatres . . .'

Sam Lane lost his licence at the Britannia in Hoxton for staging a straight production of *Black Eyed Susan*, and led a procession to Westminster with East Enders waving banners proclaiming 'WORKERS WANT THEATRES' and 'FREEDOM FOR THE PEOPLE'S AMUSEMENT'.

The East End also retaliated with the devastating weapon of mockery. At the Christmas pantomime in 1830, given at the Whitechapel Pavilion Theatre built two years earlier and one of the most splendid theatres in all of London, with a seating capacity for 3,500 people, a Major Monopoly attacked a Captain Minimus and overcame him: 'the monster enjoys but a short-lived triumph; he is in his turn attacked and destroyed to the great delight of the audience.'

Short-lived it was not, but eventually in 1843 the Royal Monopoly was broken at last. Under the new Theatres Act, which ended a hundred years of licensing madness, theatres were actually allowed to present plays. One of the first was the Britannia, re-opened by Sam Lane who told his audience: 'I am proud to have helped this success in obtaining freedom for the people's amusement. Never again will you be deprived of a free theatre.' He fulfilled his promise by staging the first British Shakespearian Festival, with the special attraction of a different Hamlet every night.

The Brit had chosen to become a theatre under the licence of the Lord Chamberlain, rather than a hall. Theatres were not allowed to serve food and drink; taverns, however, were given permission to do so, and most had a music licence, but were no longer allowed to stage 'legitimate drama'. The taverns were for the majority of people, and came between the Penny Gaffs and the posher Supper Rooms off the Strand, which catered for men. The taverns had the choice: go legit or stage the Variety which the theatres were able to abandon at last. More and more taverns chose Variety, opening a music room, concert-room, or song-saloon, in a hall beside the pub where they could also provide food and drink.

'Every publican,' wrote Willson Disher in *Winkles and Champagne*, 'would now try to lay violent hands on the building next door, whether workshop or stable yard, school or church. No opera house was too grand for the purpose and no shanty too mean.'

This was the birth of the Music Hall. Charles Morton could be called the father, for his Canterbury Arms at Lambeth was recognised as the first Music Hall in 1849. He was the first to take advantage of the 1843 Theatres Act and exploit the opportunity it presented.

As Music Hall developed, in the East End identities began to emerge. The Effingham Saloon, a favourite for sailors and prostitutes off Ratcliff Highway, became the Royal, offering 'opera bouffe' and a production of the ever-popular *Othello* with the attraction of a different Moor for every act. Hoxton, the birthplace of Marie Lloyd (of whom I shall say more in the next chapter), was rich in entertainment, which must have influenced her, if only by hearsay. The Virgo in Pitfield Street, which opened in 1867 acquired a reputation that belied the name. A.E. Wilson refers to it in his *East End Entertainment:* 'Its patrons were of the roughest kind and the hall was popularly known by a term which is too offensive to sully these fair pages. The —'s opera is as near as I can represent it, the blank being occupied by a word of similar meaning to that which Johnson in his dictionary defined as a "term of endearment among sailors".' Plainly a 'sod's Opera', a description still used for a bawdy, drunken sing-song.

Conversely, there was the smaller Macdonald's which opened as the Hoxton Music Hall in 1863, eventually becoming a mission hall which exists today, a charming hall used for the occasional Music Hall revival.

The Britannia was so grand when it was re-built in 1858 that Charles Dickens exclaimed: 'I was in an immense theatre, capable of holding 5,000 people. What theatre? His Majesty's? Far better. Royal Italian Opera? Infinitely superior to the latter for hearing: infinitely superior to both for seeing in.'

Marie Lloyd may have gone there as a child for the pantomimes presented by Sam Lane's widow every Christmas, with herself as the Principal Boy until the age of seventy-six. These pantomimes were so popular that people came

from all over London to the East End 'slums'. *King Klondyke* was seen by 260,000 people, and Mrs Lane presented such stars as Charles Coborn – 'The Man Who Broke the Bank at Monte Carlo'; Albert Chevalier – 'Knocked 'em in the Old Kent Road' and 'My Old Dutch'; and the Great Macdermott, who gave a new word to the language in 1877 with his rousing patriotic song 'We don't want to fight, but by Jingo if we do.'

Most pubs, however, seized the opportunity to present Variety in their music hall. 'By the beginning of the 1850s,' recorded A.E. Wilson, 'no public house of pretension was complete without its song-saloon, licensed for the purpose but forbidden to encroach upon theatrical preserves.'

The Grapes in Southwark was one of the first pubs with a singing-room (known as the Grand Harmonic Hall) to advertise as a Music Hall: 'SURREY MUSIC HALL Licensed Pursuant to the Act of Parliament of Geo II'. The entertainment largely consisted of song: 'Basso, Ballad, Comic, Scotch and Jacobite. Master Thompson had a New Lancashire Clog Dance to execute, and Miss Gale (daughter of the late Aeronaut) and other Mademoiselles, danced some new and favourite Pas Seuls and Pas de Deux.'

One of Music Hall's stars was Gus Elen. With his cap turned sideways, his lugubrious expression contrasted with the sharp, savage gestures of his arms worthy of a samurai. Elen spoke the language of the East End with such numbers as 'It's a Great Big Shame':

I've lost a pal, 'e's the best in all the tahn,
But don't you fink 'im dead, becos 'e ain't –
But since 'e's wed 'e 'as 'ad ter knuckle dahn –
It's enuf to wex the temper of a saint!

delivering every word with a snarling emphasis:

It's a great big shame, an' if she belonged ter me
I'd let 'er know who's who –
Naggin' at a feller wot is six foot free,
And 'er only four foot two!

This was a true cockney number, with the use of 'f' for 'th', and 'putt' as in golf instead of 'put':

Oh! [he almost squealed, judging by the scrap of
film which remains]
they 'adn't been married not a month nor more,
When underneath her fumb goes Jim –
Oh, isn't it a pity as the likes of 'er
Should put upon the likes of 'im?

and he stared at the audience in consternation, daring them to disagree.

If the loss of a pal to a wife was tragic, so was the pal who got above himself: Jack Jones who came 'into a little bit o'splosh and he dunno where 'e are':

'E says as 'ow we isn't class enuf,
Sez we ain't upon a par
Wiv 'im just because 'e's better off
Won't smoke a pipe, must take on a cigar . . .

This was the betrayal of a working man unfaithful to his mates.

The coster singer Alec Hurley (Marie Lloyd's second husband), conveyed the cockney affection for the purer countryside in 'My London Country Lane':

> Oh, I loves to take a ramble down my London country lane
> Where the nippers throw things at you and it isn't golden
>   grain.
> Though the scarlet beans and marrers
> Don't grow – they're all on barrows,
> Still, it's painted up and sez so – it's a real live lane.

On the song-sheet cover, Hurley stands there, thumbs in waistcoat in his coster's costume, the barrows behind him and the street sign 'Drury Lane' above.

This wistful wishful-thinking was expressed by Gus Elen in one of the wittiest of all the songs of Music Hall: 'If it wasn't for the 'ouses in between'.

> If you saw my little back yard, 'Wot a pretty spot!'
>   you'd cry –
> It's a picture on a sunny summer day:
> Wiv the turnip tops and cabbages wot people doesn't buy
> I makes it on a Sunday look all gay.
> The neighbours finks I grows 'em and you'd fancy
>   you're in Kent,
> Or at Epsom if you gaze into the mews –
> It's a wonder as the landlord doesn't want to raise
>   the rent,
> Because we've got such nobby distant views.

Even when I was there, East End men flocked to the flower markets on Sunday mornings, to brighten their homes, vicariously:

> Oh! it really is a werry pretty garden,
> And Chingford to the eastward can be seen;
> Wiv a ladder and some glasses,
> You could see to 'Ackney marshes,
> If it wasn't for the 'ouses in between

– the last line spat out ferociously.

Alec Hurley and Gus Elen were among many Music Hall personalities who enhanced the life of the East End who loved the East End yet yearned for a purer life. In the same tradition, the greatest Music Hall star of all was Marie Lloyd.

4

Laughter in the East End – In and Out of the Eagle

MARIE LLOYD was the essence of the East End – 'one of their own' – and epitomised the gusto of Music Hall.

The posh antecedents of Music Hall were the Pleasure Gardens. While the West Enders flocked to the splendid Pleasure Gardens of Vauxhall and Ranelagh, which charged an admission of a shilling and half a crown respectively, the East Enders had their counterparts which were elegant too, with trees, pagodas, fountains and statues, and with the luxury of space to wander in.

There were the Rosemary Branch Gardens, with the added attraction of a circus, until the tent caught fire in 1852, killing seven horses and a troupe of performing dogs. There were also the Jews Spring Gardens in Stepney, and the New Globe Pleasure Gardens in the Mile End, which sported fireworks, concerts and more ascents by balloon. Closer to the West End, the Pleasure Gardens at Sadlers Wells were especially elegant, with lakes and avenues with tables and benches under trees hung with tiny lamps. 'In the open temple,' described by a visitor at the time, 'lassies, sailors and other young people were dancing.' The entertainment lasted for three hours, consisting of a comedy, a ballet, a rope-walker, mime, balancing tricks, a strong man and an operette, during which the audience refreshed themselves with wine, ham and pasties which they placed on the shelf which ran along the back of the seats in front of them. The closest comparison I can conceive of today is the Tivoli Gardens in Copenhagen.

In particular, there was the Pleasure Grounds' Eagle Tavern; a contemporary print shows it looking especially exotic because a showman called Rouse had bought up the decorations for William IV's coronation in 1831. As an added attraction, he paid two aeronauts to ascend in a balloon and staged Devon and Cornish wrestling in the Gardens. The Eagle had a colourful past which was typical of the evolution of Music Hall: first it was a country pub called the Shepherd and Shepherdess in the 1750s, replaced by the Eagle in 1825 when the land was developed to make way for the City Road, inspiring the popular song 'Pop Goes the Weasel', in which the singer pawns his watch – 'Up and down the City Road, In and out of the Eagle.' In 1831, Rouse started to expand with the addition of the Grecian Saloon, also known as the Old Greek, with an organ and automatic piano. East Enders strolled among the coloured lights and stared in wonder at the tightrope walkers and the other attractions, as many as 6,000 in one evening. When Victoria became Queen six years later, Rouse created the Coronation Gardens surrounded by a covered walk, and a new tavern with a stage and even larger organ.

The Eagle Tavern

Audiences may have been illiterate, but this made them even thirstier for culture, with a wistful yearning to better themselves with a knowledge of the higher qualities of life. Rouse gave them opera: *The Barber of Seville* and *Don Giovanni*, which transformed the tavern into the grander Royal Eagle Music Hall. Then Rouse suffered a set-back and the land was sold to the Salvation Army, with the irony that General Booth was not allowed to pull the tavern down, and endured the frustration of seeing it prosper again with the evils of song and drink.

Marie Lloyd, whose real name was Matilda Wood, was eleven years old when Booth bought the land, and it was here that she learnt her craft. She was taken to the tavern by her father, who worked there as a waiter and was known as 'Brush Wood' because he carried a small brush and dusted himself down after serving. Under the name of Bella Delmere, she made her first appearance on the stage at the Eagle, on a Saturday night, 9 May 1885. She was fifteen years old.

Marie Lloyd was born in 1870 in Hoxton, an area which might be described as a 'slum', though an early photograph reveals that the stolid houses had a simple dignity. In spite of the poverty, the East Enders retained a local pride and the knack of bestowing evocative names. Marie's street was said to be called Peerless Street. Sadly, that was the legend and legends tend to be inaccurate: the real address, as I discovered, was more prosaic – 36 Plumber Street.

Marie's mother, Matilda, generally known as Maud, was a typical cockney, ample, humorous and shrewd. She was virtually illiterate, signing Marie's birth certificate with her 'mark', but she provided the incentive for her large, united family.

Marie, or Matilda Alice Victoria Wood, as she was christened, was the first of nine children: John, who was born the following year, 1871; Alice, who later took the name of Lloyd; Grace, who did the same; Daisy; Rosie, subsequently to appear on stage as the Lloyd family with Marie's daughter; Annie; Sydney; and Maud, born in 1890, when her eldest sister was twenty years old. Alice and Grace formed the Lloyd Sisters in 1888, to benefit from Marie's soaring reputation, though she was only eighteen.

Marie ran through the neighbourhood barefoot like the other children, and made her own entertainment, using her sisters who shared her relish for song and dance as her supporting cast, and Johnny as her audience. In those blessed days, before the all-pervading influence of television, such distraction was a necessity, particularly in the East End. Marie's extravagance was a penny-halfpenny bus ride to the cemetery at the end of the line, where she and sister Alice gawped at the pomp and pageantry so lacking in Plumber Street. On a good day they watched as many as eight funerals.

As the eldest, born to be bossy, Marie drilled her sisters into forming a minstrel troupe, highly fashionable at the time, and while her brother sold programmes the Fairy Bells toured the local missions with a sketch on the evils of drink – an ironic message in view of Marie's subsequent addiction to the stuff.

Alice was the long-suffering wife and Marie the husband who had sworn to eat his hat if he ever drank again. Crying 'Ten o'clock and he is not yet home. He will be drunk!' Alice cooked an old straw hat and served it to Marie when she staggered in, dressed in her father's coat and demanding supper.

Choking on the straw, she launched into her first song: 'Throw down the bottle and never drink again.'

'Even as a child,' said her sister, Anne Archer, 'she was always the leader of everything, not only that went on in our house but with all the kids that lived in the street.' Anne Archer told me that Marie scrubbed her sisters, including Anne herself, with such vigour in their tin bath that her mother had to object. Always adventurous, Marie explored the roofs of the neighbouring houses and found herself peering through a skylight into Mrs Schultz's kitchen next door where the German woman was frying sausages with a long, pronged fork. Looking up, she saw Marie and screamed, upsetting the fat which caught fire on the stove. Seeing the flames and the fork as if she was staring into hell, Marie started to scream as well, lost her footing, and fell through the skylight in a shower of glass, and ran out of the house still screaming.

A rare family group of the three generations: (left to right) Marie Lloyd's mother Maud Wood, Marie herself and Marie Lloyd junior

Mrs Wood tried to curb Marie's high spirits by finding her a job. The first, making boots for babies, lasted a week. At the next, the other girls dared her to dance on the table while the forewoman was out of the room, but she returned unexpectedly.

'Is this what happens when you're left alone for a moment?' she demanded.

'I couldn't very well do it while you were in the room, could I?' countered

Marie, to which there was no answer but the sack. Breaking the news to her parents that evening, she tried to lessen the damage with the announcement that she intended to go on the stage. 'At first my parents raised an objection, but when they saw that they couldn't kick their objections as high as I could kick my legs, they very sensibly came to the conclusion to let things take their course and said to me, "Bless you, my child, do what you like." '

Her parents were generous in their encouragement. John Wood took his daughter to the Eagle to watch the entertainment. She wrote,

> Every time I saw the performers dance I thought I could do better, and as for their singing, it struck me, as it does all youthful aspirants for stage honours, that my voice was superior to theirs. And in order to prove the possession of that superiority, as I could not get an audience that would pay to see me dance and hear me sing, I would get all my young sisters, even the last baby [Anne], to go into the coal cellar or up to the back attic, and have them witness my grand and expert gyrations, and listen to my beautiful voice. It must have been beautiful, for every time I sang they would all try to join with a very primitive and somewhat nasty chorus in which their yells would denote that they also possessed voices, probably not so sweet and beautiful as mine, but voices and lungs just the same. Even our blessed kid of six months old would join in and howl with delight, at least I always assumed it was with delight, till my mother would come down to the cellar and sternly ask me, 'What are you doing with the poor baby?'

Like most cockney women, Mrs Wood was house-proud – a defiance against the wretched conditions which surrounded them. Marie inherited this passion for cleanliness until it became an obsession. The more disorderly her private life became, the more the house had to be spotless: Marie would dust it incessantly, while her maids were instructed to remove any specks which dared to escape her. 'Cleanliness was a god to Marie,' recalled her sister Anne. 'Everything was always shining. "Look after the corners", she'd say, "and the middle will look after itself".'

John Wood was unambitious, though he possessed an artistic flair, making artificial flowers for an Italian who exploited him shamelessly; and though he invented a rose with a smell, which proved popular, he was paid only thirty shillings a week. This was one reason why he worked at the Eagle in the evenings. Both parents sympathised with Marie's vaulting ambition to be an entertainer. 'If my mother had gone on stage,' said Marie years later, 'she'd have shown them something. But she didn't, you see. She contented herself with bringing us up and bringing us out. She's always suggesting and criticising, is Ma.'

When she was ready to be slipped into the bill at the Eagle, her mother made her costume and she had the luck to appear with two of the leading artists of the day: Jenny Hill, 'The Vital Spark', and Herbert Campbell, who were both there for the week. Joining them for Saturday night when the atmosphere was especially lively, Marie was paid half a crown and was noticed by an impresario who engaged her to appear that same evening at the Rosemary Branch Gardens in the New North Road: 'So with another half-crown in view, I packed up my little bundle of stage clothes, slung it across my back like Dick Whittington, in search of a bloody fortune! You see, I had no nerves in those days.'

Marie soon changed her name to Lloyd, chosen by her agent who looked out of the window and saw a placard advertising *Lloyd's Weekly*; she added the 'Marie' because she thought it sounded exotic. That year, 1885, as Marie Lloyd, she appeared at the Falstaff Music Hall in Old Street, where she was spotted by a manager who placed her fourth on the bill at the Star Palace of Varieties, a popular hall at Bermondsey, after the comic Tom Leamore. Her wage packet for the week had risen to fifteen shillings. Marie was ruthlessly ambitious and stole a number from Nelly Power – 'The Boy in the Gallery', a beautiful ballad which she made a favourite of her own. Nelly died two years later at the age of thirty-two, so poor that the undertaker sued her agent George Ware for £8 19*s.* 6*d.* for the funeral expenses. Afterwards, Ware acted as agent for Marie.

As it could with Music Hall, Marie's popularity spread by word of mouth and her success was consolidated quickly. In Ireland she earned £10 a week, starring at the Sebright Music Hall in September 1886 with Sergeant Simms' Zouave Troupe, the King of Egypt, a one-legged champion, and others.

On 23 October 1886 she received her first review, after appearing at the Paragon Theatre of Varieties with Little Tich. *The Era* described her as 'a pretty little soubrette who dances with great dash and energy'.

By the end of that year she played several halls a night, followed by a growing entourage of fans, travelling by horse and brougham. Now she was earning £100 a week. In just over a year the barefoot girl from Hoxton had become a public idol and a wealthy woman at the age of sixteen. This was a transformation to which she was unable to adjust. It may explain her impulsive generosity, as if she were assuaging an inner sense of guilt over such a swift success.

Undeniably, Marie became something of a monster: a sacred monster, but monstrous nevertheless. Her private life was brazen: she took her first husband to court after he beat her up; she lived openly with the young jockey Ben Dillon while married to her second husband, the coster singer Alec Hurley; and after Dillon became her third husband she had to ask for the protection of the magistrate's court for the second time.

Because of her turbulent private life and the risqué nature of her songs, with an innuendo which could make a number like 'Oh Mr Porter' seem positively obscene, she was barred from the first Royal Command Performance held especially for Music Hall in 1912. With characteristic defiance, though many considered it impertinence, she opened her rival show at the London Pavilion down the road from the Palace, with the slogan that 'Every performance by Marie Lloyd is a Command Performance by Order of the British Public', and had herself announced as the 'Queen of the Comediennes'. When she sailed to America with Dillon, she passed herself off as his wife though still married to Hurley, and they were arrested for 'moral turpitude' on their arrival in New York and held on Ellis Island. Asked what she thought of America as she was led away, she pointed to the Statue of Liberty and exclaimed – 'I love your sense of humour!'

Even today, Marie's behaviour would be considered scandalous, yet she was the most beloved of all the stars of Music Hall. She possessed that extra 'something' and an energy barely hinted at in the few flickering seconds of film that remain of her on stage. She forged such a remarkable rapport with her audiences that they forgave her every lapse and loved her the more because of them. She represented the particular qualities of the East Enders: that defiance I have referred to and the wish to better themselves.

This was well expressed in the jaunty song in which she fulfils the popular ambition of going to France:

See the twinkle in my eye?
Just come back from France, that's why –
Me and Bill went over there to spend our 'oneymoon.
First time I'd been in foreign parts,
Did I like it? Bless your hearts!
Can't say any more than it ended up too soon.

To show that her heart still lay with the East End, she continued:

But don't think I've done with good old England – not likely.
Born and bred down 'Ackney Road, ah! an' proud to own it too.

And then, into the rousing chorus:

I'd like to go again
To Paris on the Seine,
For Paris is a proper pantomime,
And if they'd only shift the 'Ackney Road
and plant it over there,
I'd like to live in Paris all the time.

As proof of the good time she had, she asked the audience,

You like me make up?
Ain't it great?
The latest thing from Paris – straight.
Gives a girl a chance to show what she can do!

and held out the promise that they might have such luck themselves. A day-dream, perhaps, yet one of happy innocence with the solace that ''Ackney Road' was really just as good. In spite of the prevailing wretchedness, the East Ender was unashamedly patriotic. No other country was so fortunate, and she was proof that anyone could escape and reach the top.

In those days an artist bought a song-sheet outright for a few pounds, and Marie had a flair for choosing lyrics – such as the memorable couplet

Her salt tears notwithstanding,
He threw her off the landing . . .

I flinch when I hear singers screech the words of 'My Old Man' today with a meaningless gaiety, for this was not her style at all. She came on stage with a rickety bird-cage, dressed in an old straw hat and black shawl. Folding her arms, she *confided* her misfortunes to the audience –

We had to move away
'Cos the rent we couldn't pay.

Imagine the delight of the audience with the instantaneous, shared recognition, and the hoots of laughter as she cocked a snook at such disaster and laughed it away as she launched into the chorus:

My old man said, 'Follow the van,
Don't dilly dally on the way!'
Off went the cart with the home packed in it,
I walked behind with my old cock linnet.
But I dillied and dallied, dallied and dillied,
Lost the van and don't know where to roam.
I stopped on the way to have the old half quartern,
And I can't find my way home.

The lyrics by Fred Leigh told the whole sad, hilarious story.

So, at the end of her life in 1922, did those for 'It's a Bit of a Ruin that Cromwell Knocked About a Bit', the most astonishing 'character' number of all. Marie appeared as 'a relic from a bygone age', an old dear scrummaging through her handbag for a drop of gin, as she rested on a park bench. Once again she confided to the audience with a monologue before the chorus that was painfully appropriate to Marie herself, now so worn-out that her maid stood in the wings and sang the numbers with her to make them sound louder.

'Hold on,' muttered Marie, searching through her bag. 'Half a mo, I've come over funny. Here, ain't you been like it. Well, if you ain't I must have copped the lot. It's a sort of a feeling that says to you – Look old girl, it's time you had one. And that reminds me, I've got a little drop of you-know-what which does we-know-how in here . . . I shan't detain you a moment while I have a search for it . . .'

Sudden panic in her eyes as the bag swung open, revealing nothing:

'Hullo – it's gone! Would you believe it, when I came out of my house this morning I had a nice little drop of gin in here. But you can see for yourself, can't you? Bottle, cork and all gone. You know what happened to me? I've been buzzed. That's what comes from sitting in the long grass with a stranger. I'm the unluckiest girl in the world – Sooki Hardcastle; it doesn't matter what I go out with, I'm bound to go home without it.'

Then she began to sing. It is the most extraordinary song, for though the words are heartbreaking, the music has such vigour that it sounds a hymn of triumph. A nearby abbey had been destroyed by Cromwell:

> I'm very fond of ruins, and ruins I like to scan
> And when you talk of ruins, why you should see my old man . . .

In keeping with the character, she staggered as she rose:

> . . . in the gay old days there must have been some doings
> No wonder that the poor old Abbey went to ruins . . .

She staggered uncontrollably and the audience at Edmonton roared with laughter, assuming that this was part of the act, especially when she revealed that she was a victim of a pub which bore Cromwell's name:

> . . . in the Cromwell Arms last Saturday night,
> I was a bit of a ruin that Cromwell knocked abaht a bit.

Then a mad little dance, singing 'Hi-de-hi' – and she collapsed as the audience cheered. When the curtain rose the stage was empty, though the audience was unaware that it had fallen on Marie for the last time. When she died three days later on 7 October 1922, the bills were being pasted outside the Alhambra – 'Next Week, welcome return of Marie Lloyd'.

Ida Barr as a young girl. A close friend of Marie Lloyd's, she was to reveal the legend that Marie was a sacred monster

Altogether she left £7,000, to be invested for her daughter, who would receive the interest until her death, when the remainder would go to Hoxton Charities in the East End. Her funeral was one of those rare occasions when all London shares a sense of loss. Pubs were draped in black crêpe with purple cloths around the beer pumps. Twelve cars were laden with flowers, including seven hearts from the seven sisters; a horseshoe from her 'Jockey Pals'; and wreaths from every Music Hall star, including one from Clarice Mayne to 'The greatest woman of our time'. A simple bunch of flowers lay at the foot of the coffin, from her parents. Between an estimated fifty to a hundred thousand people held up the endless procession, and the crowd groaned as one car with the solitary, white-faced widower Bernard Dillon passed by.

She spanned the best of Music Hall, appealing to intellectuals as well as the East End. Max Beerbohm included her with Queen Victoria and Florence Nightingale as one of the three most memorable women of the age – 'sheer joy of living was always her strongest point.' T. S. Eliot wrote after her death: 'Although I have always admired the genius of Marie Lloyd I do not think that I always appreciated its uniqueness; I certainly did not realise that her death would strike me as the important event it was. Marie Lloyd was the greatest Music Hall artist of her time in England: she was also the most popular.'

The critic James Agate, who had compared her looks to that of 'a jovial horse', overheard a party of bookmakers returning from Kempton Races.

'She had a heart had Marie,' said one, tearfully.

'The size of Waterloo Station,' replied another.

Marie Lloyd and the gaiety of Music Hall – as well as the elegance of the Pleasure Gardens, the theatres fighting to be allowed to present Shakespeare, even the Penny Gaffs – repudiated Conrad's perception of life in the East End as 'unadorned by grace or splendour' by refusing to recognise such a dismal verdict.

5

The Whitechapel Murders

THE GREATEST reformers of the East End were the unlikeliest. Just as Hitler, by bombing the slums, gave us a rare opportunity to clear the way for a more spacious and gracious East End (which we threw away), so Jack the Ripper's influence was wholly for the good. This is not meant facetiously. Before 1888, few people entered the East End unless they had to, apart from the busybodies so preoccupied with vice, and the gentlemen and genteel ladies who collected their rents with a smile and a prayer. Policemen dared not enter the doss-house alone. One priest who did so was stripped to discover if he was a detective; finding nothing, he was kicked out and told never to return unless supplied with soup tickets. Only the Salvation Army girls, armoured by their religion, ventured on their own. The other half of London, the superior part of town, resented the reminder that people so near could live in such squalor, and ignored it, acquiring a slight sense of guilt in doing so. The Victorians had a genius for ignoring the harsher realities of life, or transforming them in their imagination into something more acceptable. For them the East End scarcely existed.

All that changed with Jack the Ripper. Inadvertently, he focused such attention on the area that the Victorians *had* to pay attention at last. This is one reason why the murders were so deeply disturbing: they exposed the terrible overcrowding in the East End, the gaiety of the Music Halls notwithstanding. Every aspect of the murders related to Whitechapel; and, although there were bad conditions in other cities such as Liverpool, none compared to those in Whitechapel and the Port of London. Now acknowledging that such conditions existed was unavoidable – as the *Daily Telegraph* reported after the murder of Annie Chapman: 'She has forced innumerable people who never gave a serious thought before to the subject to realise how it is and where it is that our vast floating population, the waifs and strays of our thoroughfares, live and sleep at night and what sort of accommodation our rich and enlightened capital provides for them.'

The Ripper's victims were easy prey. They were usually on the streets, in order to raise the sum of 4*d.* needed for a night's lodging in conditions which many of the women found so unbearable that they delayed the incarceration for as long as possible, and lingered on the outside; also, they needed the money for food. The Salvationist William Booth understood this, in spite of his stern morality, asking for help for the 'unfortunates' and 'inadequates' who:

1. having no capital or income of their own, would in a month be dead from sheer starvation were they exclusively dependent upon the money earned by their own work,
2. those who by their utmost exertions are unable to attain the regulation allowance of food which the law prescribes as indispensable even for the worst criminals in our gaols.

The skeletal horses which pulled the overladen carts through the din and congestion must have suffered, but even they were locked up at night with a bag of food and a sort of roof above. Little wonder that women such as the Ripper's victims turned to prostitution, which offered them some hope and, possibly, even some pleasure.

There were two previous murders sometimes attributed to the Ripper, and though this is unlikely their circumstances were relevant to the district.

Emma Smith, aged forty-five, described as a 'drunken Whitechapel prostitute', staggered back to her lodgings in Spitalfields around four o'clock in the morning on Tuesday 3 April 1888, after the revels of Easter Monday. Before she died in hospital twenty-four hours later, she told the police that she had been attacked by four men, the youngest about nineteen years old. She had been stabbed by a sharp instrument like a spike, and her few coins had been stolen. This seems an ordinary case of robbery by one of the gangs like the notorious Nichol Gang, which attacked prostitutes. Writing eleven years later, Walter Besant admitted in his book *East London* that

> hustling the people in the street is natural. The boys gather together and hold the street; if anyone ventures to pass through it they rush upon him, knock him down, and kick him savagely about the head; they rob him as well. In the autumn of 1899 an inoffensive elderly gentleman was knocked down by such a gang, robbed, kicked about the head, and taken up insensible; he was carried home and died the next day.

If Emma Smith's murder had not been followed so quickly by two more, all within 300 yards of each other, no one would have taken much notice.

Martha Turner (or Tabram), the alleged second victim, is of greater interest. Her murder also took place in the early hours after a Bank Holiday. Also a prostitute, she was thirty-five, but a photograph suggests that she looked considerably older, even motherly. She was married to a man called Hendrik Tabram; probably she needed the money for their rent.

On the evening of Bank Holiday Monday, Martha was seen in Limehouse with a young soldier at the Two Brewers. Later they were seen in another pub with another soldier and another prostitute. Martha's body was found on the first-floor landing of George Yard Buildings in Commercial Street the next morning. A cab driver noticed a body there at 3.30 a.m. but as this was usual he passed by. It was in the early light of 5 a.m. that another lodger, leaving for work, saw that the body was lying in a pool of blood and called the police. The doctor was startled to find as many as thirty-nine stab wounds – nine in the throat, seventeen in the breast, thirteen in the stomach. Unlike the later Ripper murders, her throat was not cut and there was no mutilation, but it seemed that the stabbing had been executed in a frenzy with two weapons at once, starting the rumour that the murderer was ambidextrous. One of the weapons was thought to be a bayonet. Surprisingly, the soldiers at the Tower were allowed to take their bayonets with them when they went out for the night, and they were lined up for an identity parade, including the two who had been seen with Martha Turner and had been arrested. The other prostitute 'failed or rather *refused* to identify the murderer', wrote a member of Scotland Yard afterwards, implying that the first soldier was guilty.

Again, little notice was taken. It was twenty-four days later that the panic started with the murder of a third woman. Mistakenly, this was associated with the others. Subsequently, it was recognised as the work of the man first known as the Whitechapel Murderer and then as Jack the Ripper.

Mary Ann Nicholls (or Nichols) was a pathetic creature, down on her luck. She was married with five children but her husband had left her. She worked as a domestic help until she stole £3 for drink and was sacked. For the last few months she had survived as a prostitute in a particularly vile doss-house in Spitalfields as her home, until even this place rejected her. Forty-two years old, short and sallow with five front teeth missing, she had little success in selling herself and on 31 August was unable to raise the 4*d*. demanded by the doss-house for her bed.

She had spirit. As she turned away, she boasted that she would earn her money and return. 'Look what a jolly bonnet I've got!' she cried. Either she hoped to sell it, or tempt an admirer – it was found later beside her body; it seems likely that she found a client, for she was able to raise a few pennies for drink. When she was seen for the last time by her friend Nelly Holland, she was almost helpless: ' "Polly" Nicholls was very drunk and staggered against the wall.' Certainly she was in no condition to resist as her murderer led her to the comparative quiet of Bucks Row where it seems that he put a hand over her mouth and cut her throat from behind. No cry, no sound at all was heard by a woman wide awake only a few yards away in one of the houses.

Her body was found at the entrance to a stableyard by a carter who thought the bundle might be a useful tarpaulin. The time was approximately 3.45 a.m. – they rose early in the East End, or returned late. Incredibly, the extent of the injuries was not realised, though her intestines protruded from her body. They were not even noticed by the local doctor, who was annoyed at being woken and barely made an examination before ordering the body to be taken to the workhouse in Old Montague Street which served inadequately as a mortuary. It was here that one of the workhouse paupers, acting as an attendant, lifted up her clothes and discovered that she had been disembowelled. The affair was bungled because the man was sick and after he had recovered he stripped and washed the body, possibly removing vital evidence.

Because murder was so commonplace it was regarded as part of everyday life and the corpses were treated with callous indifference:

'Rattle his bones over the stones
He's only a pauper who nobody owns!'

The *Star* was sufficiently shocked to describe the injuries – the throat cut in two gashes, the knife jabbed into the lower part of the abdomen, drawn *upwards* not once but twice – as the work of a maniac: 'No murder was ever more ferociously and more brutally done.'

Of all the murder sites, Bucks Row remained much the same when I went there in the fifties. The same cobbled stones and yard entrance, though the name had changed as a result of a petition from the residents, who were outraged by a postman who took macabre delight in knocking at their doors, asking 'Number 5 Killer Row, I believe?' When I went there, a few yards from the roar of Whitechapel Road shortly before it was demolished, the name was Durward Street.

In 1959, a ninety-year-old man who lived there when he was a boy, showed me the spot where the body was found. His father was another carter who got up to feed the horses at five o'clock in the morning. A crowd arrived from the factory opposite and he ordered his son to wash down some congealed blood. Yet the police officers reported that surprisingly little blood had been found; it was even suspected that the body might have been moved.

This murder attracted immediate attention because of the similarity with the other two: 'All three were of the class called unfortunates. The three murders were committed within three hundred yards of each other.' *The Times* concluded that the police believed that this was the work of one individual. That was soon to be discounted, but the first note of panic had been struck and it had a nasty consequence: a surge of anti-Semitism as the rumour spread that Mary Nicholls had been friendly with a Jew known as Leather Apron, probably a cobbler. An elderly man told me: 'I was a child then and well remember the sensation. We'd pick on some harmless old man and as many as fifty kids would pursue him ... We also called people "Leather Apron", and the local sweetshop started to make a new toffee called "Leather Apron Toffee".'

For the hunted, it was far from amusing. A Polish Jew called John Pizer was arrested at his house in Whitechapel and charged with the murder, and though he was quickly and publicly cleared by the Coroner at the inquest he was held for a further twenty-four hours for his own protection. He had the courage to sue the newspapers who identified him too soon, and, surprisingly, he won. The anti-Semitism diminished.

The next victim was equally pathetic: Annie Chapman, sometimes known as 'Dark Anne', was another prostitute, forty-seven looking ten years older, dying of consumption. Turned out of her doss-house at two o'clock in the morning when she was told 'No money, no bed', Annie gave the weary reply: 'I have not got it. I am weak and ill and have been in the infirmary.'

Her body was discovered at six o'clock in the morning in the back yard of 29 Hanbury Street by John Davis, a porter, who lived on the top floor with his wife. Sixteen people shared the small house, and the front room was occupied by a Mrs Hardman and her son, who also used it as a shop for selling cats' meat. The front door, which was never locked, led to a passage and a small yard at the end of it, frequently used by drunks and prostitutes at night.

After I moved into Limehouse, I met a charming old man who was a boy at the time. He was driving through Hanbury Street on the back of a cart when he heard the cry of 'Murder!' His natural curiosity got the better of him and he jumped off, losing his job in consequence.

'There she was,' he told me in a soft and gentle voice. 'All her entrails steamin' 'ot. And I'll never forget it because she had red-and-white stockings on.'

News of the murder spread rapidly, with the appalled realisation that this had been committed a few hundred yards from that of Mary Nicholls, and almost certainly by the same hand. Neighbours charged a small fee for a view of the back yard.

The mutilation of the corpse was even more terrible this time, though once again the body had been hosed down before a proper examination had been made. The inquest was held in the Working Lads' Institute and the Coroner complained that there was no authorised mortuary in the district, which made it 'almost impossible for a proper post-mortem examination to be carried out'. He revealed that the head had been nearly severed from the body, the body disembowelled and the womb removed; also that the further removal of the kidneys and ovaries 'showed great anatomical knowledge'.

The medical details have no relevance here, but the suggested 'anatomical knowledge' has a bearing on the identity of the man suspected by the police after the final murder, which I discovered, as I shall explain.

Surprisingly, it was the common assumption that the murderer had to be a member of the lower classes. In those days, there had to be a *motive*: passion, financial gain, anger, possibly an act of revenge after contracting syphilis from an East End prostitute. That the murderer gained his satisfaction from the act of mutilation was both unthinkable and unthought.

Queen Victoria could hardly credit that the murderer was an Englishman; certainly he could not be a gentleman. That the Whitechapel Murderer could vanish so easily added to the growing terror. Chief Inspector Abberline concluded that the murderer knew the district and its maze of passages very well, though *The Times* wondered how the man could have left Hanbury Street, 'reeking with blood, and yet ... he must have walked in broad daylight along streets comparatively well frequented, even at that early hour, without his startling appearance attracting the slightest attention.' This ignored the fact that it was light when the bodies were discovered, but dark when the murderer struck. Also, if he cut the throat from behind and stepped back, there might have been surprisingly little evidence of blood. But *The Times* drew the sensible conclusion: 'He is a man lodging in a comparatively decent house in the district, to which he would be able to retire quickly, and in which, once it was reached, he would be able at his leisure to remove from his person all traces of his hideous crime.'

However, the police looked for a working-class suspect and searched the doss-houses, though they were the first place where the murderer would have been spotted on his return. Because they were so obsessed by the image of a swarthy, black-bearded, blood-stained monster, it did not occur to them that he might have been an 'invisible man', a postman, milkman or someone else going about his everyday business and taken for granted. In this respect, the well-dressed 'toff' might be above suspicion too, on the assumption that he must have genuine business to be in the East End in the first place.

As the police seemed incompetent, and resenting the refusal of the government to offer a reward, people took the law into their own hands. Tradesmen in the East End and a local MP raised the money to offer a reward of their own, stressing the fact that to many people the East End might have been a foreign country. Wynne Baxter, the outspoken Coroner, agreed: 'There can be no question that had these unfortunate women been murdered with equal secrecy in the West End, rewards would not have been withheld.'

The *Star* advised the people to protect themselves:

> We can talk of larger reforms when we do away with the centralised non-efficient military system which Sir Charles Warren [Commissioner of the Metropolitan Police] has brought to perfection. The people of the East End must become their own police. They must form themselves at once into Vigilance committees.

The *Star* also suggested that the 'unfortunates who are the objects of the man-monster's malignity should be shadowed by one or two patrols. Whistles and a signalling system should be provided.' This became known as 'belling the cats' and did not prove popular among the 'cats' themselves, who began to notice a scarcity of clients. Nor did they welcome the suggestion that all prostitutes should be arrested after midnight, though this would have prevented one of the subsequent murders if it had taken effect.

One difficulty in finding the murderer was the lack of decoys, for there were no policewomen. A number of policemen were ordered to dress as women, which added an hilarious touch to the horror. (Another was the use by Sir Charles Warren of two bloodhounds let loose in the alleys of Whitechapel to track down the killer. Brought to Tooting Common for training, they ran away and telegrams had to be sent to all local police stations to look out for them.) One East Ender told me that his father was one of the policemen who had to dress up and was highly embarrassed because he kept his large black moustache underneath his veil. Stopped by an ambitious journalist also dressed as a woman in the hope of being accosted by the murderer, he asked him 'You're a man aren't you? Are you one of us?'

'I don't know what you mean,' replied the indignant journalist, 'but I'm not a copper if that's what you mean.'

From hell

Mr Lusk

Sor

I send you half the Kidne I took from one women prasarved it for you tother piece I fried and ate it was very nise I may send you the bloody knif that took it out if you only wate a whil longer.

signed Catch me when you can Mishter Lusk -

(Right) *A letter after the murder of Catherine Eddowes, to George Lusk, Chairman of the Whitechapel Vigilants Committee*

The idea of the Vigilance Committees, however, gained immediate public support. Even so, it seemed inconceivable that the Whitechapel Murderer should attack again in the same way in the same area. On Saturday night, 30 September, he did so – *twice.*

At this late hour the main thoroughfares like Mile End Road and Commercial Road were still teeming with people, but there were alleys off them which were emptier with dark shadows which concealed unmentionable things.

To call them a maze sounds a cliché, but is none the less truthful. In his usual effusive prose, Thomas Burke conveyed the atmosphere in *Limehouse Nights*, describing the East India and West India Docks as

> a place of savagely masculine character, evoking the brassy mood. By daytime a cold, nauseous light hangs about it; at night a devilish darkness settles upon it.
>
> You know, perhaps, the fried-fish shops that punctuate every corner in the surrounding maze of streets, the 'general' shops with their assorted rags, their broken iron, and their glum-faced basins of kitchen waste; and the lurid-seeming creatures that glide from nowhere into nothing – Arab, Lascar, Pacific Islander, Chinky, Hindoo, and so on, each carrying his own perfume. You know, too, the streets of plunging hoof and horn that cross and re-cross the waterways, the gaunt chimneys that stick their derisive tongues to the skies. You know the cobbly courts, the bestrewn alleys, through which at night gas-jets asthmatically splutter; and the mephitic glooms and silences of the dock-side.

The setting for the third murder was typical: a back yard in Berners Street off Commercial Road, where prostitutes took their clients, and must have known the cobbles intimately. At one o'clock a hawker called Louis Diemschutz drove into the yard which led to the back of an International Workers' Educational Club where he worked as a part-time steward. His horse shied violently, probably from the reek of fresh blood, for the murderer had just cut the victim's windpipe and the blood was still pouring from her throat. It is conceivable that he slipped out of the yard as the hawker jumped from his cart to investigate this bundle against the wall, and knelt appalled beside the corpse.

Imagine the murderer's frustration, for the Ripper was a sexual murderer deprived of his climax. He walked towards Aldgate, maddened by the thought of what he might have done had he not been interrupted. He was satiated all too soon. Only three-quarters of an hour later, a second body was discovered by P.C. Watkins in Mitre Square a few minutes' walk from Berners Street. His beat took fifteen minutes and he claimed he had seen nothing unusual at 1.30 a.m.

The Whitechapel Murderer had his terrible revenge: Catherine Eddowes lay on her back, her legs apart, her face gashed, her right eye damaged, her lower eyelids nicked and the lobe of her right ear was missing – fastidious touches as nasty as the mutilations. Her intestines had been pulled out and draped over her right shoulder.

It was realised with alarm that the murders were more abandoned each time, apart from the earlier interruption in the back yard. The panic was heightened when the police released a letter sent to the Central News Agency two days before the double killing:

> Dear Boss,
> I keep on hearing the police have caught me but they won't fix me just yet. I have laughed when they look so clever and talk about being on the right track. The joke about Leather Apron gave me real fits.
> I am down on whores and I shan't quit ripping them till I do get buckled. Grand work, the last job was. I gave the lady no time to squeal. How can they catch me now? I love my work and want to start again. You will soon hear of me and my funny little games.
> I saved some of the proper red stuff in a ginger-beer bottle over the last job, to write with, but it went thick like glue and I can't use it. Red ink is fit enough I hope. Ha! Ha!
> The next job I do I shall clip the lady's ears off and send to the police officers just for jolly wouldn't you. Keep this letter back till I do a bit more work, then give it out straight. My knife is nice and sharp I want to get to work right away if I get a chance. Good luck.
> Yours truly, Jack the Ripper
>
> Don't mind giving the trade name, wasn't good enough to post this before I got all the red ink off my hands curse it – No luck yet they say I am a doctor now ha ha.

This was followed by a postcard posted on Sunday 30 September, a few hours after the double murder:

> I was not codding dear old Boss when I gave you the tip. You'll hear about Saucy Jack's work tomorrow. Double event this time. Number one squealed a bit. Couldn't finish straight off. Had not time to get ears for police. Thanks for keeping last letter back till I got to work again.
> Jack the Ripper

The letter and the postcard were reproduced on a Metropolitan Police poster, asking anyone who recognised the handwriting to come forward. In spite of the macabre sense of humour and swaggering self-confidence, the police took the letters seriously and were justified in doing so, even though they inflamed the East End anxiety. No details of the double murder had been published until the Monday after the murders took place, yet the card referred to the double event and both communications referred to the lady's ears.

Even so, the writer could have learnt of the double murder by word of mouth, and guessed the rest. It is possible that the letter was a deliberate hoax

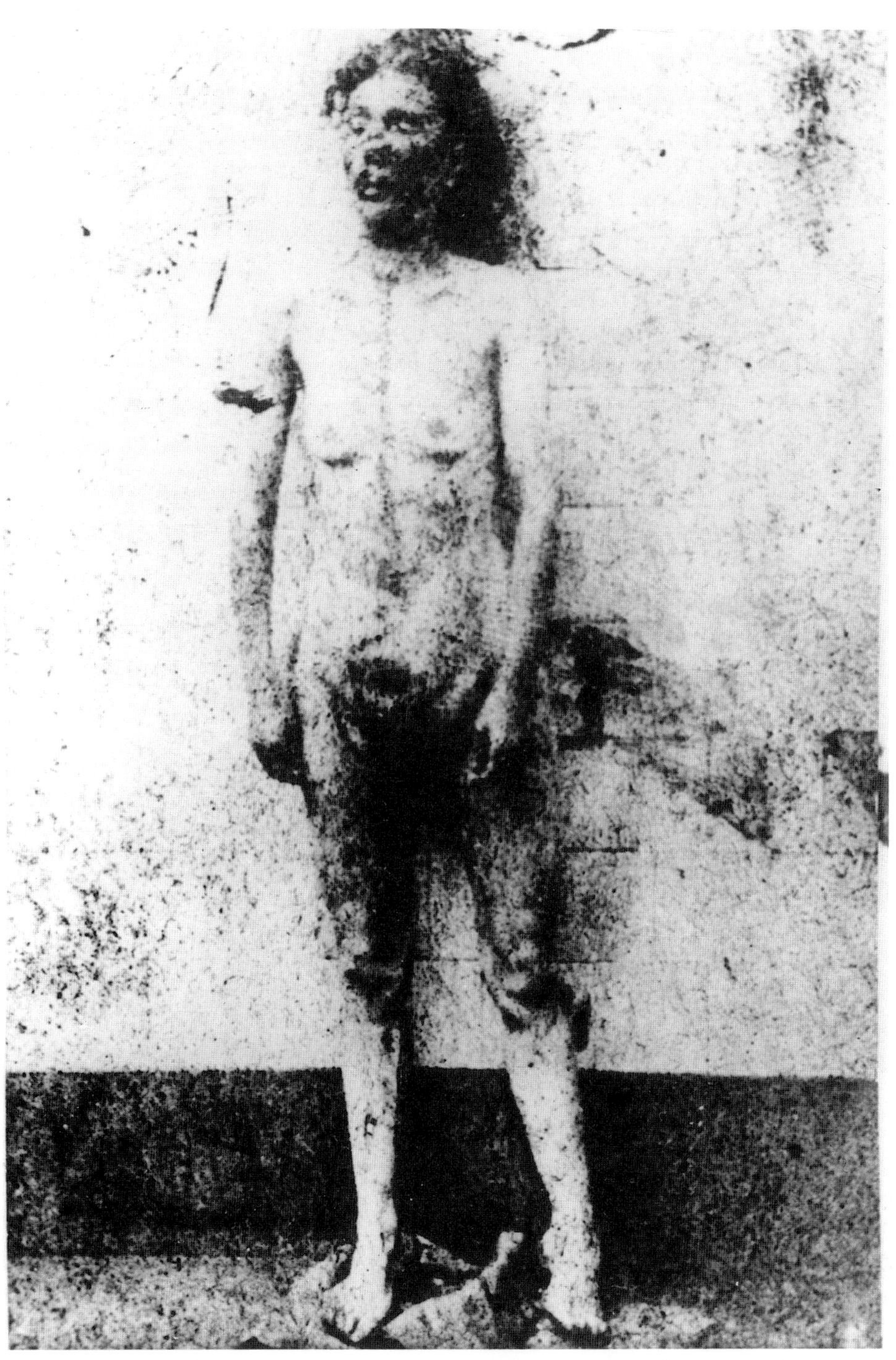

Catherine Eddowes

by an enterprising journalist who worked for the Central News Agency, and this theory was supported by Sir Melville Macnaghten, subsequently the head of Scotland Yard: 'I have always thought I could discern the stained forefinger of the journalist – indeed, a year later I had shrewd suspicions as to the actual author! But whoever did pen the gruesome stuff, it is certain to my mind that it was not the mad miscreant who had committed the murders.'

Inadvertently, by releasing the correspondence, the police gave the murderer his place in criminal history: Jack the Ripper – a name which disturbs the imagination, a hundred years later, more than that of any other murderer, even the Boston Strangler. It has been attached for an extra thrill to other murderers like the Yorkshire Ripper, and was used for years afterwards by East End families who warned their children not to go out after dark – 'else Jack the Ripper will get you'.

It was a name that was all the more fiendish because it was so awfully accurate, as I understood when the Home Office pathologist, the late Professor Francis Camps, gave me the photographs he had discovered in the archives of the London Hospital. These were of the victims, stood upright as they needed to be for the camera then, piteously exposed, the zig-zag line of rough stitching confirming exactly what had been done to them: they had been *ripped* upwards from the vagina to the throat.

The French called him *Jacques L'Evrentreur* – Jack the Disemboweller, or stomach opener. The drawings made by the doctor at the scene of the crime, the later studies made in the mortuary, and the police photographs put the claim of 'anatomical knowledge' into horrifying perspective: apart from applying the fastidious touches of the eyelids and earlobes, the murderer plunged his hand into the body and pulled out whatever he wanted. P.C. Watkins compared the body of Catherine Eddowes to that of a pig ripped up for market.

For poor, unfortunate Catherine Eddowes, her corpse suspended on the wall by pegs, the four police photographs were the ultimate indignity. There was the added irony that she had been arrested for drunkenness several hours earlier and held in Bishopsgate Police Station until she sobered up around midnight. 'Ta-ta, old cock', she said to the Duty Sergeant who released her at one o'clock, 'I'll see you again soon.' She was dead within minutes.

She fitted the pattern of the other victims: drunk and elderly at forty-three. She had, ironically, just enjoyed the respite of a few days' hop-picking in Kent: the favourite East End pastime, fulfilling the yearning for the countryside while earning a few pennies – the cockney holiday. She returned to London with the man she was living with, but by Friday they were so broke they had to separate, sharing the sixpence she had earned: fourpence for him in a doss-house, twopence for her in the squalor of the Casual Ward in Mile End Road. On the Saturday she went to borrow money from her daughter and it seems that she was successful, for she was seen at eight o'clock in the evening, staggering in the middle of the street as she imitated a fire-engine. Then she was arrested.

A description of her clothes gives an idea of the appearance of East End women of her type: she wore 'a black cloth jacket with imitation fur collar and three large metal buttons. Her dress is of dark green print, the pattern consisting of Michaelmas daisies and golden lilies. She also wore a thin vest, a drab linsey skirt, and a very dark green alpaca petticoat, white chemise and brown ribbed stockings mended at the foot with white material.' Her black straw bonnet was trimmed with black beads, and black and green velvet. This voluminous outfit was decorated with a piece of ribbon round her neck, and also 'a piece of old white coarse apron'. She wore man's boots. Her possessions, which she carried with her, were many, though meagre: 'a common white handkerchief; a blunt table knife; a match box with cotton in it; two clay pipes; a red cigarette case; five pieces of soap; a small box with tea and sugar; a "portion" of a pair of spectacles; a small comb, a red mitten and a ball of worsted'.

Identification came from two pawnbroker's tickets for a man's boots and a flannel shirt, pledged for 1*s.* 6*d.* each.

Elizabeth Stride, the third victim whose throat was cut shortly before Catherine Eddowes was murdered, was another prostitute, aged forty-five. She claimed that she came from Sweden and that her husband and two of her nine children had been drowned in 1878 when the steamer *Princess Alice* sank in the Thames, a tragedy in which several hundred people lost their lives. East Enders were still emotional about it and her story might have been invented to enlist sympathy. However, she finished up in lodgings in Flower and Dean Street, notorious for prostitution even then, and was frequently arrested for drunkenness.

In view of the tension in the East End, it is significant that the Ripper was able to pick up women with such ease. Eddowes may have been in need of money, but she had sobered up and should have been suspicious of any stranger accosting her; yet she went readily to her death in the dark corner of the square. He was either not a stranger, or someone who commanded immediate confidence like a clergyman, doctor or policeman; unless it was simply that the degradation of a prostitute's existence was such that she did not really care.

As the Assistant Police Commissioner wrote of the sensation caused at the time, 'No amount of silly hysteria could alter the fact that these crimes were a cause of danger only to a particular section of a small and definite class of women in a limited district of the East End.'

The Ripper's fifth and final victim was different: younger and livelier, only twenty-five years old. Her real name was Mary Kelly, though she preferred to be called Marie Jeanette Kelly because it sounded French and 'posh', just as Matilda Wood changed her name to Marie Lloyd. Also, she had a room of her own. Otherwise, she was a drunken prostitute like the rest. Born in Ireland, she married at sixteen and moved to Cardiff after her husband's death in a mining accident. She enjoyed a slight success in the West End theatre and claimed that she lived briefly in Paris as the mistress of one of her clients, before she went on the downward slope of the East End. She was able to rent for four shillings the small room at 13 Miller's Court, which she shared with a labourer until the end of October when she brought back another prostitute to live with them, and he moved out after an argument in which one of the windows was broken. He cared enough to return on the afternoon of Thursday 8 November to see if she was all right. That was the last time he saw her.

One of the alleys which provided a convenient cover for the Ripper's enticement and murder

Shortly before midnight, a neighbour saw her, plainly drunk, with a short, stout man; later he heard her singing 'Only a violet I plucked for my mother's grave', and noticed a light in her room. Two hours later, she was out and about once more. She met a labourer she knew near the corner of Flower and Dean Street, and asked if he could lend her sixpence, but even this was beyond him. With a smile she said she would have to find it from someone else and moved on to the corner, where she spoke to a man who put his hand on her shoulder. Laughing, they passed the labourer on their way to her room: 'My suspicions were instantly aroused,' he admitted later, 'at seeing so well-dressed a man in this part of London. I felt there was something queer about it.'

At 3.30 a.m. two neighbours heard the cry of 'Murder!' but took no notice.

At 6.00 a.m. someone heard a man's footsteps leaving the court.

At 10.45 a.m. a messenger was sent by Mary's landlord to collect the overdue rent with a warning that this was her last chance. He knocked on the door and when there was no answer he reached through the broken window and pulled the muslin curtains apart. Glimpsing Mary Kelly's body on her bed, he ran back to the landlord who called the police.

All the Ripper murders were violent, but this was the worst. Instead of ripping the body apart, he sliced her as if he was a butcher preparing trays of meat for his window, and this time he had the privacy to indulge himself at leisure. On the mattress lay a mass of raw flesh, and her throat was cut from ear to ear, though in fact the ears and the nose were missing. Her face was destroyed, her liver removed, and there was a display like a charcuterie's of kidneys, heart and slices of the victim's breasts laid out on a bedside table. It was a bloodbath. There were bloodstains on the wall and pieces of flesh dripped from the picture-rails.

I met a woman who lived in that room with her mother after the murders and she described how the police would bring visitors to show them the site of the murder and the stains on the walls which re-emerged however much they were scrubbed.

The landlord's messenger was haunted: 'I cannot drive away from my mind the sight we saw. I had heard a great deal about the Whitechapel murders, but declare to God I had never expected to see such a sight as this.' When the police joined him, Inspector Beck looked through the window and urged the young detective who was with him (who achieved subsequent fame as Chief Inspector Dew, the man who arrested Dr Crippen), 'For God's sake, Dew, don't look.' But Dew looked: 'What I saw when I pushed back an old coat and peeped through a broken pane of glass into that sordid little room which Kelly called her home was too harrowing to be described. It remains with me – and always will remain – as the most gruesome memory of my whole police career.'

It took the doctors six hours to reassemble Kelly in the mortuary into a semblance of a human being, and they found a three-month-old foetus in her womb.

With so much bloodshed, the police assumed that the Ripper had removed his own clothes. There was a small fire in the grate where they found the remains of Kelly's bonnet and some velvet in the ashes. The handle and the spout of the kettle had melted, so the fire must have been fierce.

Because of the extraordinary circumstances, there was a macabre delay in the investigation as the cheerful crowds outside thronged towards the Lord Mayor's Show in the City, on a rare excursion to the West. Commissioner Warren's instructions were that no murder site should be touched until his bloodhounds were ready, so, as if mesmerised, the police waited for his arrival. At eight that night, they learnt that Warren had resigned, a decision which was greeted with cheers when it was announced in the House of Commons a few days later. Another victim of the Ripper, though scarcely mourned.

Bursting open the door, the police superintendent arranged for two remarkable photographs to be taken: the first, which I published for the first time after it was given to me by Professor Camps, showed Kelly on her bed, though it takes time to realise that this was once a woman. The other, one of the last orders from Warren, echoes the brilliant short story by Rudyard Kipling *At the End of the Passage* which demonstrates the belief that a final image is retained on the retina of the eyes. Warren hoped that a photograph of Kelly's eyes would reveal the murderer, but it proved as ineffective as the two bloodhounds, Barnaby and Burgho.

The murder of Mary Kelly marked the end of Jack the Ripper. After such violence, no further murder could satisfy his lust. He could resume a normal life, which would not have been true to character, or take his life, if the police failed to catch him. He could not continue.

Before I explain my discovery of his identity, I should say more of the Ripper's relevance to the East End, which took various forms. The Penny Dreadfuls exploited the sensation in the purplest prose – 'Horror ran throughout the land. Men spoke of it with bated breath, and pale-lipped women shuddered as they read the dreadful details. People afar off smelt blood, and the superstitious said that the skies had been of a deeper red that Autumn.'

Hoardings became so gruesome that they were denounced by *Punch*, and the newspaper boys enjoyed a field day. 'No one who was living in London that Autumn will forget the terror created by these murders,' wrote Sir Melville Macnaghten. 'Even now I remember the foggy evenings and the cries of the newspaper boys, "Another horrible murder, murder, mutilation, Whitechapel."'

Though fear of the Ripper became a shared experience in the East End, like that of the Blitz, the place resembled a wilderness at night. A publican in Whitechapel went bankrupt: 'People aren't going out any more,' he explained. 'Since the killings I hardly get a soul in here of a night'; and this was confirmed by a letter to *The Times*: 'I and a friend last night made a tour of the district ... and in spite of what we had been led to believe, found the district almost deserted.'

Far from causing disinterest, the events increased public sympathy towards the East End: as a result of the murders, people learnt that death from starvation was commonplace, and that 55 per cent of children died before the age of five. As a gesture, the American actor Richard Mansfield withdrew his production of *Dr Jekyll and Mr Hyde* from the Lyceum with a final benefit performance to raise money for the homeless. 'Experience has taught this clever young actor that there is no taste in London just now for horrors on the stage,' declared the *Daily Telegraph* approvingly. 'There is quite sufficient to make us shudder out of doors.'

Bernard Shaw, then a thirty-two-year-old dramatic critic, sounded his blast in the *Star* under the heading 'Blood Money to Whitechapel':

> The riots of 1886 [a dock strike] brought in £78,000 and a People's Palace. It remains to be seen how much these murders may prove to be worth to the East End ... Indeed, if the habits of Duchesses only admitted of their being decoyed into Whitechapel backyards, a single experiment in slaughterhouse anatomy on an aristocratic victim might fetch in a round half million and save the necessity of sacrificing four women of the people.

The Lancet noted that the crimes had been committed 'in precisely the same district where, as sanitary reformers, we have often demanded the intervention of the authorities'; and the *Star* even posed the possibility, 'too horrible to contemplate, that we have a social experimentalist abroad determined to make the classes see and feel how the masses live'. 'Who is my neighbour?' asked *The Times.* 'Unhappily for all of us, the Whitechapel murderers and their victims are neighbours of every Londoner.'

Such rhetoric alone would have been scant consolation to the East Enders themselves, but now the words were backed by royal endorsement. Queen Victoria rebuked the Home Secretary – 'The Queen fears that the detective department is not so efficient as it might be' – and after the murder of Mary Kelly she sent a stronger telegram to her Prime Minister: 'This new most ghastly murder shows the absolute necessity for some decided action. All these courts must be lit, and our detectives improved.'

The Survey of London (Vol. XXVII) acknowledged that the murders 'undoubtedly gave a further impetus towards the rebuilding of the Flower and Dean Street area', while Mrs Henrietta Barnett, the energetic wife of the Vicar of St Jude's, claimed 'Verily it was the crucifixion of these poor lost souls which saved the district.'

So the Ripper's victims had not died in vain, achieving with their death more for the East End than all the Secretaries of State throughout the century.

6

How I identified Jack the Ripper

NATURALLY, I tried to learn all I could about Jack the Ripper after I moved into Limehouse. He was still a legendary figure and I met a few survivors who remembered the events of 1888.

Later, I appeared on television to ask for information on the Ripper; it was probably the first time this had happened. I was inundated by letters, some of which were hoaxes, many which were mistaken, and a few which were genuine. I thought my luck was in when I met a delightful old lady who had been in service as a young girl and was sent by her mistress to fetch sixpence-worth of fish for the master's supper. Running down the street, Annie charged straight into Jack – 'And there he was,' she told me in a voice still awestruck, 'with his big black beard and his black bag with all those knives ready to cut me up. And he had a little black moustache. My son, he do make me laugh, says, "It was Charlie Chaplin, Mum!" I forgot all about the fish and was scolded by the mistress, but I wouldn't go out again, and didn't, on my own, for ever such a long time in case I saw him again.' Her brush with death was the high spot of her life. Sadly, my questions revealed that her dates were confused, and the event had occurred *after* the murders, but I did not disillusion her.

I learnt from her in other ways, having tracked her down to a pristine house in a new town on the outskirts of the East End, a suburb of dreadful dullness and conformity. I spoke to her in a spotless room and when we were alone she told me how much she hated it. This was the first time that I appreciated how much the slums were missed by those who grew up in them, as she talked forlornly of the close companionship she had known. She looked as out of place as a wax fruit under a glass dome.

Perhaps they were saved by the innocence of ignorance, for they did not know any better, but the drab little houses did not mean that their lives were drab – anything but. Also, living cheek by jowl, they were bound together, their doors unlocked, as Annie's wistful yearning for the past illustrates.

My discovery of the Ripper's identity came by chance.

I was staying in North Wales with Lady Rose Maclaren, who asked me what I was working on. When I mentioned the Ripper, she explained that this was a lucky coincidence, for we were due to visit her mother-in-law, the Dowager Lady Aberconway. Her father was Sir Melville Macnaghten who joined Scotland Yard as assistant chief constable in 1889, and became the head of the Criminal Investigation Department in 1903. As he joined the Yard so soon after the murders it was part of his job to close the file on Jack the Ripper, and he made his private notes at the same time. Shortly after his death, his daughter copied his notes and was kind enough to give them to me after my visit that afternoon in 1959. They revealed to me the identity of the man suspected by the Yard at the time. This was the proverbial 'scoop', though I scarcely realised the extent of it.

There were three suspects. The first two were predictable – a mad Russian doctor and an insane Polish Jew with a hatred for women. Writing of the third, Macnaghten conceded:

> I have always held strong opinions regarding him and the more I think the matter over, the stronger do these opinions become:
>
> *Mr M.J. Druitt*, a doctor of about forty-one years of age and of fairly good family, who disappeared at the time of the Miller's Court murder, and whose body was found floating in the Thames on 3 December, i.e. seven weeks after the said murder. The body was said to have been in the water for a month, or more – on it was found a season ticket between Blackheath and London. From private information I have little doubt but that his own family suspected this man of being the Whitechapel murderer; it was alleged that he was sexually insane.

I was faced with the challenge of playing detective myself with a further investigation nearly seventy-five years later. The task was aggravated by several mistakes made by Macnaghten: at first no such doctor could be found, no record of such a body drowned in the Thames that month, no record of such birth or death in the archives of Somerset House. For a confusing week, it seemed that Macnaghten had named the wrong man.

Then my researcher and I made a break-through with the discovery of two physicians called Druitt, one of whom proved to be Montague's father. Macnaghten had made two vital mistakes: Druitt was thirty-one, not forty-one, and he was not a doctor but a rather unsuccessful barrister. His corpse had been found on 31 December but had not been registered until 2 January in the following year, which is why we had been unable to confirm it in 1888. Now the pieces began to fall into place.

Montague came from a good family, brought up in Wimborne in Dorset where his father, Robert, was one of the county's most respected men: a Justice of the Peace, a governor of the grammar school, 'a strong Churchman and Conservative', and a distinguished surgeon.

Montague was educated at Winchester College where he won a scholarship to New College, Oxford. When he entered the law he kept chambers at King's Walk, though he rarely received a brief. By 1888 he was teaching as an assistant at a private school run by George Valentine at 9 Eliot Place in Blackheath. Once a school of some distinction, it was by 1888 a 'cramming shop' with forty-two boys as boarders, three masters, a cook and six servants crowded into the building. Druitt still kept his chambers at the Temple.

The one area of his life where he seemed successful was on the cricket field, which would have proved a considerable asset as assistant master. Indeed, Colin Wilson doubts that Druitt could have been guilty because in his view no cricketer could commit murder. For some reason, never disclosed, Druitt was sacked by Valentine, apparently around the time of the last murder.

The full story of Druitt has been related elsewhere, especially by myself, but having explained the Ripper's impact on the East End in such detail it seems only right to outline the conclusion of the story.

When I discussed the murders with the pathologist, Dr Keith Simpson, he was adamant that the Ripper could not have been a doctor because his lust would have been satiated by his work or noticed by his colleagues. Yet he was convinced that the murderer had some medical and anatomical knowledge. This fits Druitt, whose father and uncle were surgeons; and he grew up in a medical ambience with easy access to such medical instruments as a post-mortem knife, generally considered to have been the murder weapon.

I made a further discovery which seemed crucial: that his cousin, Lionel Druitt, also a doctor, had a surgery at 140 Minories, a minute's walk from Mitre Square where Catherine Eddowes met her death. Could Montague have stayed with his cousin? This would explain his knowledge of the district and how he 'vanished' after the killings. My excitement evaporated when I learnt that Lionel had emigrated to Australia in 1887 *before* the murders, but this in itself proved to be relevant.

Trying to trace a document – *The East End Murderer – I knew Him* – by Lionel Druitt or Drewett, referred to in one of the letters sent to me, which was printed privately by a Mr Fell of Dandenong in 1890, I tracked down the source on a visit to Australia in 1961 and met an elderly lady who remembered Dr Druitt who lived in nearby Drouin but then the trail went cold.

It was possible that the letter was a hoax; but if it wasn't, what evidence could have justified Lionel Druitt in making such a claim when he was out of the country, unless he had some 'inside information'? The answer was supplied in January 1973 in the *Cricketer*: an unlikely source, apart from M.J.D's distinction in the game. Irving Rosenwater discovered that Captain Edward Druitt, Montague's younger brother, departed for Australia early in 1889 – 'an unusual procedure for a regular officer' – and Rosenwater assumed that Edward acquainted Lionel with recent facts known to the family and was glad 'to remove himself from the scene of potential embarrassment in England'.

This is guesswork, but the existence of Edward and his three sisters is significant, due to the perjury of their elder brother's evidence at the inquest on Montague. Though William Druitt was a reputable solicitor in Bournemouth he testified that he was the *only surviving relative*, apart from their mother Anne. He gave her as the reason for his brother's suicide, substantiated by the note he had left behind: 'Since Friday I felt I was going to be like mother, and the best thing for me was to die.'

Anne Druitt was confined to a private asylum in July 1888 two miles north-east of Whitechapel, and if Montague had visited her at the weekend from his school at Blackheath, he would have travelled through Whitechapel at a period in his life when his mind would have been disturbed by her condition.

William lied. Why, unless he had something more terrible to hide? Macnaghten made his conclusion: 'I have little doubt but that his own family suspected this man of being the Whitechapel murderer.'

Macnaghten concluded that Druitt drowned himself 'after his awful glut [when] his brain gave way altogether.' Conversely, Druitt could have left Miller's Court that morning, mingling with cheerful crowds on their way to the Lord Mayor's Show, satiated yet empty with the realisation of what he had done, and, unable to endure his guilt, taken his own appalled and appalling life.

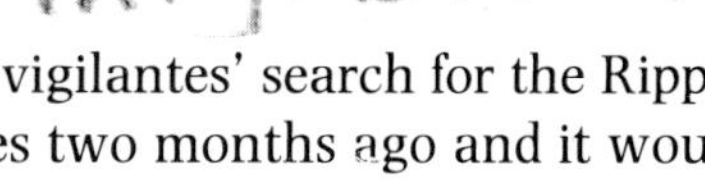

One fact is undeniable: in March 1889, the police visited Albert Bachert, the founder of the Whitechapel Vigilance Committee, and told him he could call off the vigilantes' search for the Ripper because he had been 'fished out of the Thames two months ago and it would only cause pain to relatives if we said any more than that.' It is worth noting that identification of guilt has been suppressed in other cases since then, if the family were half as respectable as the Druitts, and the murderer deceased.

There have been numerous theories, clues which were red herrings, even *The Final Solution* by the late Stephen Knight which proved to be a hoax. I am more convinced than ever that Druitt did it. When I showed him the evidence, Professor Francis Camps wrote to me: 'The Killer's identity established. I am sure this is the answer at last.'

I have to admit that I climbed on to a bandwaggon, and even took the reins for a time, and that more nonsense has been written on the Ripper than on any other criminal. The speculation reached its lowest point in 1988 when the anniversary of the murders turned into a media celebration.

I have scant sympathy for feminists, but I can understand their rage when the Jack the Ripper public house in the East End, a particularly unsympathetic place which has since been renamed, sold a cocktail called the Ripper Tipple and sold T-shirts emblazoned with the Ripper's victims.

Reformer he may have been, though inadvertently, but also one of the most callous killers in criminal history who did not deserve such celebration.

7

My skirmish with the Krays – a sentiment of villains

SHORTLY AFTER my arrival at Limehouse, someone invited me to the opening of a club in the Mile End Road called the Kentucky. Though I remember the place today as a small bar, it was transformed that night into a lavish 'venue' complete with stage, so hectic, amplified and overcrowded that it was difficult to speak.

This was my first experience of East End glitter. Everyone was immaculately dressed, the men in dark-blue suits, dark ties and white shirts, the women with elaborately structured hairstyles. I was impressed, especially when Billy Daniels appeared on the makeshift stage and gyrated his energetic version of 'That Old Black Magic'. Unless my memory is wrong, both the local mayor and vicar were present, and I was introduced with a flourish, as a new arrival, to the owners of the Kentucky, two smart young men with a surprising similarity to each other, described as 'civic businessmen'. These were the Kray twins. When they asked me if they could add my name to the committee, along with that of the said mayor, vicar and other dignitaries, I was happy to agree, flattering myself that such a gesture marked my acceptance by the East End.

I doubt if the local police ever believed that someone could be so ingenuous. A high-ranking officer, a superintendent or inspector – I was so unconcerned that I did not even notice, called at Narrow Street a few days later to suggest tactfully that it might not be in my best interest to appear on the Kentucky Club notepaper as a member of the committee. This could lead to trouble, he suggested. When I asked him why, he flinched from telling me the risk in forming an association with the Krays, understandably reluctant to reveal the extent of his own knowledge. I had no idea of the Krays' activities whereas he was immersed in them, as one of the policemen who were trying to bring them to trial. Both of us were puzzled by the need for such a visit and he left me none the wiser, though I agreed to withdraw my name from the committee. This did not amuse the Krays at all. In fact they were highly miffed when I told them, demanding to know exactly what the police officer had told me. Equally bemused by my naivety, they withdrew into an uncomfortable reticence of their own. After this my name was removed and the incident forgotten.

As I had no reason to suspect the Krays, I made no notes and took no photographs. There is one occasion which mystifies me today as I try to recall it, and I cannot place the date exactly, but I remember being taken to a large sporting club in the East End called the Double R, where the Krays were present though I did not know of them then, with the strong impression of being unwelcome, regarded as an outsider. However, I was told that it would be much appreciated if I could use my influence to raise the case of a man who had been wrongfully convicted. Perhaps I could do so on television. I refused, and sensed a disapproval. The thought occurs to me now that I was being asked to intervene on behalf of Frank Mitchell, 'the Mad Axeman', who had been rescued from Dartmoor, hidden by the Krays in London and, so the rumour went, subsequently killed. No body was found but it has been suggested that the remains of this unfortunate, simple-minded man are encased in one of the concrete blocks which support the Hammersmith motorway.

What perplexes me is not so much my stupidity, for I have never underrated that, but my indifference to such events. If I sensed danger at the Double R club and recognised the risk of becoming involved with a villain who was 'on the run', and if the police came to warn me after my visit to the Kentucky that it was unwise to be associated with the Krays, why on earth did I continue to know them instead of veering off as far as possible?

Though it seems inconceivable, I believe it was due to a total lack of fear, bred from ignorance. I exuded no musk of apprehension because I did not feel it, and because of this I was safe, for the Krays did not know what to make of me. It could have been as simple as that.

Also, the Krays and the Kentucky amused me. God help me, I rather liked them. It is curious how the title of 'gangster' has a touch of glamour, evoking the bootlegging days when rival gangs gunned each other down in Chicago. When Al Capone attended a baseball game, the crowd cheered him. Then Hollywood immortalised the racketeers in the gangster films in which they were portrayed and, to a degree, glamorised by Raft, Bogart, Edward G. Robinson and Cagney; even when they came to their inevitable sticky end, the sympathy of the audience stayed with them. Now we have a film on the Krays. 'Villain' was another title commonly used in the East End, yet so melodramatic, so redolent of bygone days with knights in armour and damsels in distress that it was hard to take seriously. 'Murderer' was a word that no one mentioned, not even the police officer who called on me, and, in my naivety, it did not occur to me that the Krays were capable of such a crime, though I gathered vaguely that they were guilty of 'protection'.

Because I was unfamiliar with the rituals of the East End, and not yet aware of the liveliness of pubs, I spent several lunchtimes at the Kentucky Club and once I witnessed the legendary violence. A young East Ender took the considerable risk of chatting up Reggie Kray's girlfriend, and was soon invited outside – an invitation that could not be refused. The two men withdrew to a small back yard where they proceeded to fight, in full view of us, with a squaring up of bare knuckles, fancy footwork and general fisticuffs as deferential to the Queensberry Rules as anyone could wish. When honour was satisfied, they shook hands, wiped off the blood, put on their jackets and resumed their drinking at the bar. This was *Gentleman Jim* stuff and I was enthralled, never having seen such a fist fight before.

But if the image of the Krays had scant effect on me, by God I baffled them! When I lurched down the stairs of an evening, Ronnie Kray would sigh, 'Have a care, Daniel, there's ladies present. Do mind your language, please.'

This was the irony which appealed to me, that the Kentucky was prim. The customers were well turned out; the villains smartly dressed and the women had gone to considerable trouble to 'get themselves ready'. The banquettes were covered with simulated white leather and the walls with red Regency flock. This was why I introduced Joan Littlewood to the club when I acted as her adviser on the film *Sparrers Can't Sing* (an experience I shall describe in due course). Perhaps it was an inverted snobbery on my part, but it puzzled me that she failed to see the humour of such gentility at the end of the Mile End Road. I was dismayed when she transformed the Kentucky for the filming into a sleezy club with a gum-chewing tart in a split skirt smooching to an imported jukebox, for this was not the Kray twin style at all. They looked on unhappily but said nothing, for they had taken an instant liking to Joan Littlewood, with the empathy which sometimes exists between villains and show-biz 'personalities'. She responded, calling the Krays 'lovely villains' to their faces, or 'my lovely couple of clowns'. I flinched at this at first, but they seemed to like the attention. Indeed they were photographed constantly, standing unsmilingly in group photos which included such stars as Danny La Rue, all of whom were smiling madly, and nice, bubbly Barbara Windsor who had problems of her own with her husband Ronnie Knight, another East End villain, who was to leave her later and settle in Spain, somehow avoiding extradition.

It was arranged that the world première of *Sparrers* should be held in the Mile End cinema opposite the Kentucky, with the proceeds going to a Dockland Settlement charity which ensured the presence of Her Royal Highness, Princess

Margaret. This was a gala occasion for the East End and the Krays in particular, who booked the Dress Circle for themselves, their families and henchmen. I remember seeing them that evening, pale and strained in dinner jackets and none too pleased to see me, for I had neither ticket nor evening clothes. There were more 'heavies' surrounding them than I had ever seen before.

Their ill humour was aggravated by the sudden cancellation of H.R.H., who was suffering from 'diplomatic flu' (my phrase) after someone at Kensington Palace had the wit to realise that she would be surrounded by the entire Kray organisation, and thereby lend them credibility. Or, the Palace could have been alerted by the police inspector who had come to Narrow Street. Princess Margaret was represented by Lord Snowdon, who performed the honours handsomely and spoke to the cast afterwards, but I sensed that the Krays were disappointed not to brush with royalty, and rather hurt.

After I had a succession of burglaries, for Narrow Street was highly vulnerable from the riverside, the Krays suggested that I needed a 'minder' as a non-paying lodger in the attic, and I agreed. Ted – the said minder – was humorous when he wasn't sulking, with a sharp appreciation of the absurdities of life and a cheerful cockney wit. Some people thought him slightly mad, which was certainly true of his companion, Fritz, a Doberman who had been attacked with a brick by his previous owner, rumoured – as I discovered later – to be one of the Krays themselves. Devoted to Ted, who was equally devoted to him, Fritz hated the rest of the world apart from my mongrel bitch Littlewood, with whom he was so infatuated that he followed her everywhere, drooping visibly when she refused to acknowledge him. Their relationship was startling, but if he was fearsome, she was fearless.

One Sunday morning Fritz raced into my room and leapt on the bed, wriggling and barking with sudden pleasure as dogs are apt to do. Delighted to discover that Fritz was canine after all, I reached out to stroke him, but in an instant his fangs were bared and his hackles rose as he growled at me threateningly, while I had the sense to remain motionless until he ambled off.

Fritz terrorised my housekeeper until her husband told me she would leave unless he was locked up, and he alarmed a newly arrived neighbour to such an extent that she complained to our landlady about 'the beast next door'. When Dolly Fisher understood that this woman was referring to a dog, rather than myself, she came to Narrow Street to investigate. I was out and Ted opened the door. Fortunately my housekeeper was there so Fritz was duly locked up. With remarkable presence of mind, Ted produced Littlewood instead, who played her part by jumping up ecstatically, smothering Mrs Fisher with kisses.

'Can't think what she's on about,' said Ted innocently.

'Nor can I,' snorted Dolly Fisher, depositing the joyful puppy on the floor. 'I'll phone that woman and tell her she's mad!'

Another incident was less agreeable. Ted took Fritz for long walks in Victoria Park and they returned one afternoon highly pleased with themselves: 'Fritz met this 'orrible, yapping little terrier, didn't he, would have torn him to pieces till I called him off. Still had a good bite, didn't you, Fritz,' he said, patting the dog's battered head affectionately. 'Blood everywhere, ruddy woman screamin' her head off until I told her to stop or I'd give her one.'

My God, I thought, I need a minder to protect me from my minder.

I experienced another twinge when it occurred to me that the Krays might be using Ted as a 're-minder' sent to collect their gambling debts. This was confirmed when the artist Lucian Freud arrived in Narrow Street one morning to buy back an unfinished portrait he had sold me a few weeks earlier. I knew of his obsessive gambling but had no idea that he patronised Esmeralda's Barn, a smart gambling club in Knightsbridge where the Krays were 'joint partners'.

Plainly it came as a nasty shock when the door was opened by Ted who seemed unpleasantly familiar to Freud. Equally surprised to see Freud, with money in his outstretched hand, Ted respected the East End code of hospitality, while I tried to overhear their muttered words and promises. Ted emerged with a sly smile and Lucian looked paler than usual – a vampire trapped in the sunlight. However, such incidents did not phase him and we never referred to the encounter afterwards.

There is no denying that the Krays treated me impeccably. When I ran my pub on the Isle of Dogs, which I shall describe in due course, and I saw them less often, Ronnie told me, 'You know we wouldn't come to the pub without an invite, Dan.' I was wiser then and did not extend the invitation, responding with a vague smile as if I had no idea of the implications involved. Scrupulously polite as always, his deep, dark eyes expressionless, the 'Colonel' accepted this. I did not owe him money. Only my tongue could have offended him by 'taking liberties' and there must have been moments when I was in danger of losing it. Otherwise, by his rules, I had not transgressed.

Always keen on the limelight, which was ultimately to destroy them, I believe they wanted me to write their life story, but I no longer wished to be involved now that I knew the truth. I regret the lost opportunity now for the Krays exemplified the honour-bound code of the East End: the honour among villains which kept to a strict set of rules, where no one talked out of turn and a 'grass' was someone to be disposed of. They had the additional human bondage of identical twinship: they were born within an hour of each other in 1933. The tendency to glamorise the twins as the Robin Hoods of the East End has the fallacious romanticism of the photographer who finds beauty in the ugliness of the slums (I admit my own blame in this respect) but they had their moments of bravado which confirmed them as local heroes. In a district where boxing or crime was an easy way out, the twins settled finally for the latter – 'There is something sexy about crime,' Reggie explained to a friend.

In particular, they were much admired for the escapade when Reggie visited his brother in Epsom Prison for the Criminally Insane where he was being detained after a case of GBH – grievous bodily harm. While Reggie stayed inside, Ronnie walked out in his twin's mackintosh and stayed on the run for two weeks before giving himself up when he found a Harley Street psychiatrist prepared to certify that he was sane. Together, the twins looked different, with Reggie leaner and keener, but it was hard to tell when you met them separately. Usually they were inseparable.

Ronnie did not conceal his preference for boys – 'Little angel faces, less evil-minded than girls'. A young friend of his listed the virtues of the Krays to the artist Francis Bacon, who listened bemused:

'They're good to their muvver.'

'Yaas?'

'At Christmas they send more than 300 cards to their mates inside.'

'Do they really?'

'And when a member of the Firm goes inside, the Colonel sees they get flowers sent to their wives . . .'

The roll of honour continued until Bacon could bear it no longer:

'Fair touches the heart!' he exclaimed.

'It does, doesn't it!' said the delighted, wide-eyed boy.

The twins voiced their contempt for petty thieves and blackmailers of homosexuals at a time when such an activity was against the law, and they contributed generously to local benefits, raising money for such charities as the Aberfan disaster and Amnesty International. Conversely, they received large sums of money from their protection of small bookies and illegal gambling clubs, and debt-reinforcement for shady car-dealers. If they had possessed the wit to stay discreetly in the background, appearing to go straight while others took the rap, they might have become accepted as 'civic businessmen' who were millionaires. They could not resist the risk and they enjoyed the celebrity, which was part of their vaulting ambition. As John Pearson, one of their first biographers, explained: 'There is a vast and unlovely innocence in the way this doomed pair proceeded on their grandiose and disastrous way. For none of the violence which finally, and incredibly late in the day, turned the organised energy of Scotland Yard against them was logical nor even remotely necessary.'

Idolised in the East End as local boys made good, albeit bad in the process, they came to the notice of the West End gradually. Their role at Esmeralda's Barn seemed legitimate and they were doing good business – £1,000 a week in 1960.

The incident which brought the Krays to the attention of the public for the first time concerned the rumours of a photograph which showed a well-known 'peer of the realm' in the company of notorious gangsters, with the implication of a criminal relationship. Various names were bandied about in private, for the affair was highly libellous with its implication of homosexuality and crime, until a Sunday paper published the photograph in question of Lord Boothby seated smilingly between the twins. I have been told that Boothby was in the south of France when someone phoned him the news as he was sitting down to lunch. Returning to the table he danced with delight – 'Now they've identified me, I can sue. This is what I've been waiting for!' And sue he did.

Though the British public were mystified by the Boothby scandal, which seemed more smoke than fire, the name of the Krays became suddenly familiar. London seemed closer to Chicago and the days of old-fashioned 'gangsters' and Prohibition.

A week or so later I was invited to a party given by Judy Garland at the Boltons. It was a splendid party with good food and drink and interesting people, yet not too crowded; Garland was radiant and hospitable. I was enjoying myself thoroughly talking to Danny La Rue and the leading show-business solicitor, the late David Jacobs, when Jacobs paled beneath the heavy make-up he adopted which gave him the startling appearance of being Chinese.

'My God!' he whispered. 'Look who's just come in.'

I turned round and there were the Krays, with Ronnie escorted by a bodyguard. I learnt later that this was not to protect Ronnie, but to protect the guests in case he gave way to one of his increasingly mad fits of violence, which I had been spared until that moment.

I was not surprised to see the Krays, assuming that the American mafia – who overrated them – had put them in touch with Judy Garland, as they had with Billy Daniels earlier.

The Krays had boasted to the writer Francis Wyndham of such relationships: 'George Raft – there's a nice man. He's well-respected [in fact the Home Office barred him entry to Britain in 1967]. A very smart man – he's *immaculate*. And he still dances a lovely tango. Sophie Tucker – she was a very nice woman, done a lot for charities. She used to work in speakeasies when she started, knew such people in her time as Al Capone. She said he was a nice fellow, Al Capone, a greater gentleman you couldn't hope to meet, she said.' So it was hardly surprising that the Krays wished to meet Judy Garland, even if she had little idea of what they represented.

There was a hush in the conversation as they entered. After looking around the guests for someone he recognised, Ronnie Kray came towards us and to my dismay spoke directly to me, in a voice of such frigidity that it chilled my blood.

'Hullo, Dan. Long time since I see you. Last time you blagged me something rotten.'

'Did I?' I squeaked, not sure if an apology would make it better or only serve to aggravate. The 'minder' hovered expectantly near by. At this moment I was saved by the interruption of a sweet, little, grey-haired lady, one of the caterers supplied by Harrods, who entered the room with a deafening cry – 'Mr Reginald Kray, is there a Mr Reginald Kray? If so, he's wanted on the telephone.'

With the recent publicity concerning Lord Boothby and the gangsters, there was consternation. She could not have created a louder silence if she had called out 'Mr Capone? Mr Al Capone? There's a Mr Dillinger on the line.'

Ronnie Kray moved on accompanied by his minder, and that was the last I saw of him.

During my years in the East End I became friends of the Barry brothers who ran the Regency Club near Stoke Newington. I knew them well enough for one of the brothers to confide in me one evening that he was becoming involved with the Krays and wanted to get out. Could I help him with a loan? I refused for the simple reason that I did not have that sort of money, and we lost touch after I left the East End and moved to Devon. I had no idea how closely John Barry was involved, but on 6 March 1966, he accompanied Ronald Kray as they walked into a pub called the Blind Beggar in Bethnal Green.

Inside the pub was George Cornell who had been a friend of the Krays, though he worked for the Richardson gang, most of whom were now inside. Ronnie had sent some fruit to Cornell's son in hospital a few days earlier, but Cornell warned the father of Ronnie's nineteen-year-old boyfriend, referring to Ronnie in public as 'a fat poof'. This was the provocation needed for Ronnie to establish his authority by killing a man who was drinking on his territory and 'deserved to die'. At 8.30 p.m. the bar of the Blind Beggar was almost empty apart from Cornell, and Barry emptied it entirely by firing at the ceiling while Ronald Kray drew a 9 mm Mauser pistol and shot Cornell above the right eye. 'Ronnie does some funny things,' said Reggie when he heard the news.

With the code of the East End that was honour bound not to 'grass', there were no witnesses. Not even the barmaid could tell the police who was responsible. The Colonel had exerted his authority so successfully that he returned to the Blind Beggar with immunity, ordering a 'Luger and lime' at the bar.

Intoxicated by his performance, he taunted Reggie into committing a murder of his own. Jack McVitie, a small-time crook who perpetually wore a hat to cover his baldness, was chosen as the victim after it was reported that he, too, had spoken out of turn. On 29 October 1967, the Krays and members of the Firm arrived at the Regency Club and told John Barry that they were going to kill 'Jack the Hat' on the premises. He implored them not to and they moved to a basement near by, leaving two henchmen, the Lambrianou brothers –

further proof of the East End criminal fraternity – to escort McVitie to a 'party'. As soon as he entered, Reggie pushed him against the wall and pulled the trigger, which misfired. As McVitie fought for his life, Reggie put the gun to his head and fired again, but nothing happened. To cries of encouragement from Ronnie, he took a carving knife from one of the men present and stabbed McVitie through the throat, so violently that the blade came out the other side, into the floorboards where McVitie was lying.

Again, none of the violence 'was logical nor even remotely necessary'. This was killing for kicks, and in doing so the Krays had put themselves beyond the pale. To ask why they committed murder is to judge them by normal standards, but Colin Wilson gave a perceptive insight when he wrote in *A Criminal History of Mankind*, referring to the Krays in particular, that 'In the last analysis, the criminal is a Peter Pan, a child who refuses to grow up.' Some Peter Pans!

The end, as described by Pearson, was macabre, with Ronald Kray in vest and slacks in his ninth-storey council flat in a tower block, sitting on a Dubonnet-coloured sofa as he stroked 'the head of a young male boa-constrictor' ordered from the pet department in Harrods. Probably he recognised that he was about to endure the ultimate celebrity – arrest, trial and imprisonment. In May 1968, under the supervision of Commander John du Rose, a squad of sixty-eight policemen made surprise raids at dawn in various parts of the East End. They found Reggie in bed with a blonde girl, and Ronnie with a young man.

Eleven men stood in the dock at the Old Bailey in January the following year, including John Barry. A list of charges included the murders of Cornell, McVitie and the Mad Axeman, Frank Mitchell, though his body had disappeared.

The prosecution eventually withdrew the charges against Barry and he was released. The Krays were sentenced to thirty years each, with the irony that they earn more than £1m a year today, from the sale of T-shirts, books and films, far more than they did from crime. In February 1990, they sacked their publicity representative because he was encouraging the wrong image. Today, Ronnie Kray is confined to Broadmoor.

The last word should go to Arthur Mullard. We were taking part in *This is Your Life* for Queenie Watts (of whom, more later) and had reached the last small room before the studio. As we waited for our call, he said 'You knew the Krays, didn't you?'

'Yes,' I replied vaguely, rehearsing what I was going to say in a moment's time. And then I resorted to the most banal of all the clichés applied to Ronald and Reggie: 'I quite liked them. After all, *they only killed their own kind.*'

Arthur Mullard looked at me stonily. 'Yuss,' he nodded, *''uman beings.'*

One of my early photographs of Petticoat Lane

8

THE PORT AND THE GHETTO

WHENEVER I COULD, I would spend hours on my balcony, where I absorbed the passing of the river, fascinated by its unfamiliarity as if I had reached a foreign city instead of the heart of London where I was born. For me it seemed as strange as Istanbul.

I began to recognise the features: the mud flats opposite with flights of gulls which rose, whirling and screaming when a small boy searched for loot, like a former mudlark. I looked for the foreign flags and the names on the stern to identify where the ships had come from, with a growing affection for exhausted-looking cargo-boats, like old French women dressed in black whose tired faces tell everyone that they have been carrying things for too long.

I began to recognise the characters: like the huge Irishman called Murphy who stood upright in his tiny launch and controlled the monopoly in buying and selling rope – a monopoly which was confirmed by the size of his fists. Even when it rained he was hard at work, scuttling from one side of the river to the other, with a sack pulled over his head for protection. A threatening figure in the tradition of Rogue Riderhood who searched the Thames for bodies in Dickens' *Our Mutual Friend.*

I learnt that London was still one of the busiest ports in the world, in spite of the damage to the docks by Hitler's bombs. The recovery was proving slow, but at least the leading docks were active, half a dozen of them, starting with Tilbury twenty-six miles down river, then the Royal Docks, the West India and East India Docks near by, and the London, Surrey and St Katharine Docks near Tower Bridge. Two hundred thousand passengers passed through the Port of London, extending 92 miles upstream from the Thames Estuary to Teddington, in the course of the year; what a splendid way to arrive in England, disembarking in the shadow of the Tower of London.

The river-pilots brought the vessels to Gravesend where Her Majesty's Customs and Excise came on board, after which they were escorted up river by one of the fleet of waiting tugs.

I was reminded of the days I had spent walking along the dockside lined with swaying, empty ships when I tried to join the Merchant Navy, and my departure and return to Tilbury when I succeeded. I felt in touch with the sea once more.

By day I explored the docks from the water, racing down to Greenwich in my Dowty jet-boat, and once even to Gravesend, or purring slowly up Regent's Canal or the River Lea, where all was silence apart from the murmur of the engine, while grime-stained, deserted warehouses loomed over me.

At night the river acquired a peace of its own at low tide, and all I needed on my return was to lean over the balcony and feel every tension fade within me.

Narrow Street, previously Fore Street and Limehouse Street before that, had been interspersed with small shipyards since the time of Queen Elizabeth, and an early map of London in 1703, when Limehouse was separated from London by marshland, shows the shore dotted with docks below the houses where the captains lived when they came ashore while their ships were repaired below them.

Mr Sennett outside his seaman's outfitters, near the Eastern Hotel, armed with a cricket bat, presumably against a possible attack after the murder of his wife on the same premises

In 1816 a woman called Clementina Black recorded her impression of 'The houses on the south of Narrow Street [which] look out upon the river. Many of them have bow windows and little wooden balconies and steps running into the water. Some of the rooms are low and small and have about them an odd suggestion of a ship's cabin. As we go down the wooden stairs, the blue stretch of the river spreads before us ...' Later Dickens described a similar atmosphere: 'In and out among vessels that seemed to have got ashore, and houses that seemed to have got afloat – among bowsprits staring into windows, and windows staring into ships.'

I found it much the same, though I was surprised by Clementina Black's reference to 'the blue stretch of the river'; I doubt if Dickens would have recognised this description either. By the middle of the nineteenth century, the river was already polluted, as the song-sheet for *The Lamentation of OLD FATHER THAMES*, sung at Public Dinners by Mr Hudson and Mr Taylor, shows. The cover by William Heath illustrates a tattered Neptune rising near

St Paul's with a dead cat impaled upon his trident. He is surrounded by evidence of pollution with humorous captions: a prostrate eel – 'murder most foul'; 'ghosts of departed flounders'; 'whitebait looking black'; and Neptune himself, exclaiming 'Here's a mefs [sic] I am in'. When I arrived, you were advised to have your stomach pumped out if you fell in the water; the idea of catching a fish there was unthinkable.

The West India Docks were opened in 1802 to ease the problem of the congestion of ships unloading in the river, for this was chaotic, with mass looting taken for granted, though the locals were dismayed by the arrival of armed guards who patrolled the high walls of the dockside.

A free-water clause allowed the lightermen who unloaded and loaded the ships to take their barges into the docks without paying a due. When the West India Dock Company tried to revoke this in 1900, pleading a shortage of space, they were opposed so bitterly in Parliament that the Port of London Authority was formed a few years later to cope with such matters, and the PLA supervises the river to this day. Its launch, *The Havengore*, was chosen to carry Sir Winston Churchill's coffin from the Tower to the quay at Waterloo.

Yet the docks brought strife. There were always too many men after too few jobs – 600 men to 20 jobs in the 1880s – in spite of the number of ships docking, and they were paid so miserably, at $2\frac{1}{2}$*d.* an hour, that many fainted from hunger even if they succeeded in getting employment.

With so many foreign ships entering the port, it was inevitable that the sailors who poured ashore in the last century – and were frequently decanted back unconscious – added to this district's character. Many of them headed for the White Swan in Ratcliff, known locally as Paddy's Goose, described by the American writer, Daniel Kirwan, as 'perhaps the most frightful hell-hole in London'. Kirwan found no honest merriment:

> The very sublimity of vice and degradation is here attained, and the noisy scraping of wheezy fiddles and the brawls of intoxicated sailors are the only sounds heard within its walls. It is an ordinary dance house, with a bar and glasses, and a dirty floor on which scores of women of all countries and shades of colour can be found dancing with Danes, Americans, Swedes, Spaniards, Russians, Negroes, Chinese, Malays, Italians and Portuguese in one hell-medley of abomination.

Such a colourful mix of nationalities sounds glorious – the closest I have come to it was Flower Sellers Alley in Istanbul before it was cleaned up – but even the Bohemian De Quincey, with his taste for opium, found it offensive: 'Manifold ruffianism shrouded impenetrably under the mixed hats and turbans of men whose past was untraceable to any European eye'.

Yet there were other sailors who went inland in search of higher entertainment, and the influence of the London River permeated the halls and theatres such as the Pavilion, Whitechapel, which presented 'nautical drama' – indeed it was advertised as 'The Great Nautical Theatre of the Metropolis'. The audience relished such productions as *The Sailor's Home* with 'naval engagements and picturesque tableaux'. *The Referee* described an audience in 1883: 'It is perhaps the most cosmopolitan pit in the Metropolis. Here may be seen the bluff British tar; the swarthy foreign sailor fully arrayed in picturesque sash, a red mop-cap and a pair of earrings; the Semitic swell in glossy broadcloth, and the rorty coster, a perfect blaze of pearly buttons . . .' – a kaleidoscope of the Port of London in the 1880s with the 'Semitic swell' as the antidote to Fagin.

One of the grandest theatres was the Standard at Shoreditch, destroyed by fire in 1866, which rose again as 'the largest and most magnificent Theatre in the world' where every leading actor appeared, even Sir Henry Irving. With so many illiterates in the audience, spectacle was popular: one show included a genuine horse-race that galloped across the stage from the wings on one side, into Holywell Lane on the other, while a policeman stopped the traffic.

Totally forgotten, this was the tragic façade of the Pavilion Theatre when I moved into the East End

Ballet astounded with 150 fairies floating in mid-air; and the Nautical Dramas included a representation of the sinking of the *Princess Alice* in the Thames (in which Elizabeth Stride, the Ripper's third victim had claimed she was a survivor), with dead bodies laid out on stage while small boys recreated the waves by stirring about under a painted canvas. The tragedy was still remembered with considerable emotion.

Swelling the influx of sailors and those connected with the sea, came the immigrants from Eastern Europe seeking a greater permanence. They came in such numbers that their arrival ran the risk of racial riots as they began to overwhelm the area around Whitechapel in particular.

By 1854 the Jewish population for all of London had reached an approximate 25,000–30,000. Most of these lived in the East End. As the pogroms in Eastern Europe grew more oppressive, the Jews escaped in increasing numbers – 1,636 Russian refugees in 1891; 3,277 the following year; up to 5,000 in 1913 when the annual immigration came to a halt with the outbreak of war. Afterwards, there was a period of abeyance until a new generation of Jewish refugees left Nazi Germany while they still had time to do so.

The Jews from Eastern Europe were desperate, illiterate, and many never learnt to speak English though they stayed in the East End for the rest of their lives. Several people told me that as children they wandered through Spitalfields and seldom heard a word of English.

The first arrivals were taken to a temporary Jewish shelter in Leman Street which opened in 1885, where food and accommodation was arranged for them. A Jewish Free School started near Petticoat Lane, there was an orphanage near by, and a soup kitchen was set up off Brick Lane which still remains with the old, stone lettering above the door – 'SOUP KITCHEN FOR THE JEWISH POOR' – though largely patronised by old-age pensioners today who receive their soup in tins.

An example of the Jewish ability to adapt is given by Edith Ramsey in the booklet *This is Whitechapel* which accompanied the exhibition of outstanding photographs by Ian Berry at the Whitechapel Art Gallery in 1972. She described how the new arrivals kissed the ground, 'for they knew they would be safe and able to follow their religion', and quoted the case of Jacob Fine, an undersized Jewish boy who came alone from Poland. As the boat steamed into London, the gates of Tower Bridge opened, which impressed the fifteen-year-old boy considerably, but once on shore he was mislaid, overlooked by the Jewish welfare workers who received immigrants, and he stood there alone, unable to speak a word of English. After his experience in Poland, he feared the worst when the police descended, but they gave him thickly buttered white bread and sweet tea at Leman Street Police Station before they led him to the Jews' Temporary Shelter. It would be nice to think that this friendly reception influenced the rest of his life, and perhaps it did, for Jacob Fine became the

Secretary of the Jewish Tailors and Garment Workers Union, and a leading member of the Stepney Borough Council. He received the OBE before his death in 1970.

By 1900, it is claimed that 100,000 Jews had settled in and around Whitechapel. This concentration was due to the restrictions imposed on foreigners who tried to live within the City walls, though Greeks, Italians and French settled further west in Soho. The pressure of such an alien population in the middle of the English East End could have been overwhelming; somehow it was contained. The Jews were bound together by their faith, which remained intact. The Hebrew faith meant that they looked after themselves with gifts of bread, meat and coal for the poorest among them, without resort to the harsh Poor Law, greatly feared in the East End and by the Jews in particular with their horror of unearned money. Many preferred to starve than become an extra burden on the rates; begging was regarded as a crime – boys who hawked matches in the City were punished if they were caught – while domestic service, a happy release for many Christian girls, was disapproved of. The Jews even kept to themselves in marriage, regarding an association with the gentile as degrading. Prostitution was condemned, so they did not present a threat sexually.

Traditional undertaker opposite Limehouse church

Determined to make their way, the Jews worked all hours – often through the night – and formed a separate ghetto. Understandably the first generation was grateful to the country which had accepted them. The trouble often comes with the second generation who lack the all-consuming challenge of adapting to a new culture, and turn to crime, as the sons of Italian migrants did in New York and Chicago. This did not happen here. Preoccupied by their work, the Jews began to flourish as furriers and tailors, specialising in every aspect of the rag-trade – adding *schmutter* to the language. When they prospered, some moved away – others were proud to remain. They began to expand with their own library, bank, post office, a Yiddish Theatre in Commercial Road, and numerous small kosher restaurants. On Sundays, after I arrived at Limehouse, I went to the Jewish market in Hessel Street to stock up for lunch parties.

As workmen, they created their own crafts, excelling at tailoring, but even here they kept themselves separate, as W.J. Fishman explains in his definitive book on the East End in 1888 – 'A Year in a London borough among the labouring poor', which gives a detailed examination of the East End in that particular year.

W.J. Fishman stresses that the Jews 'formed their own self-contained street communities, a precarious livelihood eked out in small domestic workshops, their ethnic unity perpetuated within their *stieblech* – small, house-based synagogues catering for the spiritual and social needs of the *landsleit* (families emanating from the same village or town in Russia or Russian Poland.)' Within such confines, the workshop conditions may have approached sweated labour, but that was their decision and the choice of the Christians who worked for them, apart from the fact that employment was hard to find outside. They were not feared as competitors.

Even so there were outbursts of anti-Semitism from boys who threw stones at passing Jews because of their unfamiliar clothes and beards, and residents who objected to crowds of 'foreigners (our co-religionists)' clogging the footpaths on Saturday nights. The indefatigable Fishman quotes many well-publicised attacks on the Jews. There were also those who should have known better, like the magistrate who revealed his ingrained prejudice when he asked, 'Why doesn't the man speak for himself?'

'He is a native of Poland.'

'Then let him go to Poland,' said the magistrate loftily, in an exchange more fitting to the Music Hall.

By 1888 the writer Charles Booth was able to record that 'The newcomers have gradually replaced the English population in whole districts which were formerly outside the Jewish quarter ... their fate independent of the great stream of London life surging around them.' This intrusion by the 'newcomers' was often resented by the older-established Jews who came from different backgrounds and had long since been assimilated, such as the Dutch, known for manufacturing cigars, and the Germans, known for baking bread and tailoring. The term 'Jew' was too simple, considering the various levels it embraced.

The older-established Jews might well have agreed with the *Jewish Chronicle* after an incident on 18 January 1887, during a late show of the operetta *Gypsy Princess* at the Yiddish Theatre in Princes Street, when someone in the gallery cried 'fire'. Though this proved a false alarm, or a hoax, seventeen people were crushed to death in the ensuing stampede, including twelve women and four children. Implying that the 'self-imposed alienation from English society' of such newcomers was responsible, the *Chronicle* warned that:

> One of the most direct causes of the recent disaster has been the persistent isolation in which they have kept themselves from their fellow Jewish workmen in all the social amenities of life. When they want aid in sickness or distress they are willing to claim their privileges as Jews living in England, but in all their social relations they keep aloof from us, and thus forego the advantages of such an institution as the Jewish Working Men's Club where every practical precaution has been taken to avoid such a calamity as the late panic. The recent event ought to be a lesson to avoid such performances of strolling minstrels acting in the jargon, and helping to keep up the alienation of the foreign contingent.

The newcomers found themselves in a situation where they were bound to lose: if they stayed in their ghetto they were condemned for their 'aloofness', if they moved out, they became a threat. Indeed, the growing fear that the newcomers *would* overwhelm the residents prompted a House of Lords committee to hear evidence with a view to stopping further immigration by an Act of Parliament. Much of this evidence has an uneasy parallel with the problems of immigration today.

Even the Anglo-Jewish Conservative candidate for Bethnal Green, Arthur Sebag-Montefiore, expressed his alarm at a pre-election meeting: 'this is an extremely delicate subject for me to discuss. While I cannot bring myself to refuse our free shores to persecuted foreigners, I would do all in my power to dissuade these foreigners from coming to our shores', while Captain Colomb, the Conservative MP for Bow and Bromley, spoke out more forcibly in the House of Commons, asking:

> What great states of the world other than Great Britain permit the immigration of destitute aliens without restriction; and whether Her Majesty's Government is prevented by any Treaty obligations from making such regulations as shall put a stop to the free importation of destitute aliens into the United Kingdom.

The Pall Mall Gazette had raised the alarm earlier in February 1886, warning of 'A Judenhetz brewing in East London ... foreign Jews of no nationality whatever are becoming a pest and a menace to the poor native-born East Ender'; but the bigot in this explosive woodpile was a man called White, though his views were so extreme that he enlisted sympathy towards the very cause he was attacking. At one point he paraded a cross-section of Jewish immigrants to confirm their squalor before the House of Lords committee, only to be exposed as a fraud, for the entire exercise had been arranged by an agent called Levy who promised local Jews that if they 'presented themselves as ill-clad and starving "greeners" they would be aided by a funding Committee either to return them to their homeland or to be shipped further on to the real Promised Land – the United States.'

Captain Colomb returned to the fray with his statement to a reporter that he objected to 'England with its overcrowded population and small area being made a human ashpit for the refuse population of the world', and Arnold White continued his campaign, undeterred, joining a deputation to Lord Salisbury in February 1888 urging the government to take action 'to prevent the wholesale immigration of destitute persons into this country'. The deputation included the Rev. Billing, a holier-than-thou clergyman who was Rector for Spitalfields, who bewailed the sight of 'half-starved miserable Jewish children on the streets, picking up the garbage from the gutters and bearing all the traces of disease ... It would be a real kindness to prevent them from coming here.'

Faced with such prejudice, the Jewish Board of Guardians tried to defuse the situation by keeping it quiet, and seized on the chance to encourage immigrants to continue to New York, which extended a warmer welcome – judging by the inscription on the Statue of Liberty:

> Give me your tired, your poor,
> Your huddled masses yearning to be free,
> The wretched refuse of your teeming shore,
> Send these the homeless, tempest-tossed to me.

I should point out that 15,000 of the tempest-tossed were refused permission to land and ordered back to Europe. Unfortunately the same inhumanity applied here, and W.J. Fishman quotes the report in the *Jewish Chronicle* of 'a score of poor, woe-begone Russian Jews' sent back to Hamburg by the Jewish Board of Guardians: 'One aged woman some eighty years of age, particularly created pity, and in the early hours of Saturday morning one of the Christian ladies on board started a collection on behalf of the poor dame, and about 22*s.* were handed to her, much to her surprise and gratification at this last mark of charity of the English people.' Or hypocrisy. It was even suggested that immigrants should be repatriated to their homeland, regardless of possible persecution, with their fares paid for by the Board of Guardians (a parallel to the suggestions to curb coloured immigration today).

There is no doubt that the prejudice against the Jews, even apart from the bigotry of such campaigners as Arnold White, was severe. The Rev. Billing, of Spitalfields had no hesitation in confirming it when he appeared before the House of Lords committee. After protesting in his sanctimonious manner that he should be sorry to 'prejudge these people by a sweeping accusation', he continued by doing exactly that, with his assertion that the Jews 'had no knowledge of the decencies of life ... Whole streets were occupied by Jews where there was not a Jew before. If a Jew got into one room he soon got a Jew into another and it became intolerable for the Gentiles to remain ... The Jew did not like the Gentile, and the Gentile did not like the Jew.' The overcrowding was undeniable – there were tragic cases of so many children sleeping in a bed with their parents that the youngest were likely to be 'overlayed' and suffocated to death – but the Rev. Billing was as bigoted as White, in his more sinuous way. His charge was promptly rebutted by the Chief Rabbi who said he had seen 'Christians labouring with perfect content in the Jewish workshops'.

But resentment of the Jews gradually abated, and they had their champions – although these sometimes tended to be as romantic as their opponents were bitter, with a Liberal writing to the *Pall Mall Gazette* in 1888: 'Their emaciated, sickly frames are the stamp of martyrdom. There is a halo of holiness around them which every true Christian must recognise and respect.' Surprising as it may seem, the true East Ender was strong enough to afford such tolerance, while the newcomers were warned by established Jewish residents to 'Eschew your Yiddish language and culture. Adopt the English language with its civilising customs!'

Another champion was Margaret Harkness who described the Jews of Spitalfields in her sentimental novel, *In Darkest London*:

> buxom Jewish matrons sat on doorsteps, watching the little dark children who tumbled at their feet. Young Hebrews smoked short pipes and talked their own lingo. Now and then a young girl with jet black hair and flashing eyes ran by, carrying a loaf of German bread under her arm, singing a foreign song or jodelling. There was nothing English about the place, only foreign faces, foreign shops, foreign talk. The Jews looked happy, although they were in a strange land, exiles as their fathers were, crowded into the narrow compass of the East End ghetto. They had not the down-trodden look of our Gentile population, which seems to enjoy crouching and whining instead of asserting itself with a sturdy independence.
>
> The Jews have, it is true, long-suffering faces, but they have hope written in their features, instead of that despair which seems to sadden English East End men and women. Perhaps this habit of looking towards Jerusalem

> accounts for this, for the synagogues of the East End show men and women full of religious purpose. The down-trodden Gentiles seem to have lost their faith; they speak of death as 'the great secret' while the Jew classes death 'God's kiss', even when it comes to him in the crowded dens of sweaters or the filthy rooms which he shares with newcomers from the Continent.

This implies that the Jews brought that touch of *glamour* to the East End, found wanting by Joseph Conrad, and though this might sound as if I am stretching a point in order to prove it, this is reinforced by W.J. Fishman, who knows more about the subject than anyone alive, with the benefit of his own Jewish background:

> the collective experience and tenacious adherence to their ancient culture endowed the Jews with such qualities as inspired hope, even pleasure albeit ephemeral, within a life of adversity. Their religious ethos, with its accompanying sense of personal fulfilment expressed through traditional communal practice within and without their *stieblech*; the weddings and *simchas* (family celebrations); the emotive *barmitzvahs* and the close-knit family concerns; the picaresque Jewish eccentrics who stalked the main streets of the ghetto to exhort, instruct, but always to entertain . . .

Fishman concludes: 'all these and past historical imperatives would bind them together with indissoluble ties.'

Gradually the resentment abated. The absorption of the Jews into the East End of London is an astonishing and salutary example of tolerance. Even during the scary months of Jack the Ripper's murders, a time when all classes came under suspicion, the anti-Semitism was minimal.

After the First World War there was a period of abeyance when the numbers of immigrants decreased, until it swelled again in the 1930s as Jews fled from Nazi Germany. In 1936 Oswald Mosley marched down Cable Street flanked by 3,000 of his supporters and the usual glum-looking policemen in their unhappy role as guardians of a militant minority. The newsreels reveal the confrontation: Mosley's blackshirts, confronted by a motley variety of men who belonged to different religions but were bound together by the district they belonged to: Irish, who came here after the potato famine, Jews, and other East Enders. Many were dressed identically in a raffish uniform of their own – cloth caps, white shirts and kerchiefs. Violent fighting broke out and people were hurt, but Mosley was turned away. This was one of the most triumphant moments in the history of the East End. Mosley was a brilliant politician, yet he had failed to understand the nature of the district or the common sympathy of those who lived there.

Ultimately, the cohesion of the East End had proved greater than its parts.

Walter Besant, another chronicler of *East London* (1903) let loose a colourful

flight of fancy when he noticed that the newly arrived Polish Jew was a man of poor physique:

> he is a small, narrow-chested, pasty-faced person.
>
> 'Is this,' you ask, 'a descendant of Joshua's valiant captains? Is this the race which followed Judas Maccabaeus? Is this the race which defied the legions of Titus?'
>
> 'My friend,' replies a kindly scholar, one of their own people, 'these are the children of the Ghetto. For two thousand years they have lived in the worst parts of a crowded city; they have been denied work, except of the lowest; they have endured every kind of scorn and contumely. Come again in ten years' time. In the free air of Anglo-Saxon rule they will grow; you will not know them again.'

And so it came to pass.

The Docks – A Night Scene *by Gustave Doré*

9

THE LAST VESTIGES OF CHINATOWN

AFTER LADY ABERCONWAY gave me her father's notes which helped me to identify the man suspected by the police as Jack the Ripper, she sent me a copy of *Limehouse Nights* by Thomas Burke, a popular bestseller on its publication in 1916 though scarcely remembered today.

I did not appreciate the book at the time. Probably I leapt on it too eagerly in my search for background material, and was disappointed by the exotic tales of Limehouse which were hearsay or pure invention. Finding the prose too florid, I failed to see that this is the virtue of the writing, as true to the exotic nature of Chinatown as James Elroy Flecker's *Golden Journey to Samarkand*.

Reading the stories today, I find my reaction inexplicable. What an opening! Burke introduces the story of 'The Chink and the Child':

> It is a tale of love and lovers that they tell in the low-lit Causeway that slinks from West India Dock Road to the dark waste of waters beyond. In Pennyfields, too, you may hear it; and I do not doubt that it is told in far away Tai-Ping, in Singapore, in Tokio, in Shanghai, and those other gay-lamped haunts of wonder whither the wandering people of Limehouse go and whence they return so casually. It is a tale for tears, and should you hear it in the lilied tongue of the yellow men, it would awaken in you all your pity. In our bald speech it must, unhappily, lose its essential fragrance, that quality that will lift an affair of squalor into the loftier spheres of passion and imagination, beauty and sorrow. It will sound unconvincing, a little ... you know ... the kind of thing that is best forgotten.
>
> Perhaps ...
>
> But listen.

With all the talk of yellow men, Chinks and Niggers, his book would not stand a chance of being published today, but how richly Burke evoked the magic of Chinatown in days when such words were used naturally. The tales of betrayal and vengeance sought by those betrayed are stylised and the 'twist' at the end as predictable as a deduction by Sherlock Holmes, and as satisfying. Burke conjures up a cast of characters worthy of a musical: bullies like the boxer Battling Burrows and Hunk Bottles; Chinese lovelies like White Blossom, and pale girls – Gracie Goodnight and Pansy Greers; and 'that masculine lady', Tidal Basin Sal. Or the loathsome, scrofulous 'doper' Tai Fu.

Inevitably, the love between the Chinese men and the Limehouse girls ends in starkest tragedy, as if it were doomed. Cheng rescues the pathetic Lucy, known as White Blossom, from the clutches of Battling Burrows who destroys her after he learns that she has gone with 'a yellow man'. Cheng reclaims her:

> From Pekin Street to Pennyfields it is but a turn or two, and again he passed unobserved as he bore his tired bird back to her nest. He laid her upon the bed, and covered the lily limbs with the blue and yellow silks and strewed upon her a few of the trampled flowers. Then, with more kisses and prayers, he crouched beside her.
>
> So, in the ghastly Limehouse morning, they were found – the dead child, and the Chink, kneeling beside her, with a sharp knife gripped in a vice-like hand, its blade far between his ribs.

Battling staggers back from the Blue Lantern to Pekin Street and flops heavily on his bed:

> So, when Battling flopped, eighteen inches of writhing gristle upreared itself on the couch, and got home on him as Buf Tuffit had done the night before – one to the ear, one to the throat, and another to the forearm.
>
> Battling went down and out.
>
> And he, too, was found in the morning with Cheng Huan's love-gift coiled about his neck.

Burke's stories may sound romantic rubbish in such emasculation, but he conveyed the vulnerability of this tough Eastern neighbourhood.

In contrast to the Ghetto, with thousands of Jews inside, Chinatown was a delightful aberration containing a few hundred Asians who arrived at the West India Docks after a long sea journey, and stayed there or returned.

I was fortunate to witness the last vestiges of Chinatown, though the Chinese lettering was already cracked and peeling on the shuttered shop-fronts and the legendary area was little more than a final façade. A courteous Chinaman with skin like faded parchment showed me around the club in Pennyfields called the Chun-Yee where the members played Mahjong, and I drank in the Commercial on the corner of West India Dock Road near by where I heard more Chinese than English and did not feel particularly welcome. I ate in the Old Friends in Mandarin Street which heralded the New Friends and the Friendly House, run by Mr Lo-Cheong and Mrs Farmer, and their beautiful, smiling Eurasian daughters.

Otherwise I had to rely on memories. Limehouse residents told me of the pukka-poo gambling cards, like an early form of football pools, and the labyrinth of small houses interlocked by passages, so when a Chinaman ran from the police into a house at one end of the street, he was likely to emerge in another street altogether. In contrast, the East Enders marked the progress of the rent-collector as he knocked on doors along their street by the families who scuttled into their back yards until he had gone.

I learnt also of the Chinese funerals, lavish affairs with food placed on top of the grave.

'Why waste good grub like that?' asked a cockney wit. 'You think 'e'll rise up and eat it?'

'Why you put flowers?' replied the Chinaman impassively. 'You think 'e come up and smell 'em?'

Sadly, the opium dens were features of the past, except when referred to by the passing pleasure boats as they approached Limehouse. *Opium!* what an exotic image is conjured up, especially when attached to *den*; a 'Laudanum Saloon' would sound sedate by comparison. Many Victorian gentlemen were addicted to this form of opium, including Dickens, and used it for purposes which were neither medicinal nor sedative. Where alcohol served as an obliteration, opium and laudanum offered the promise of oblivion.

In *The Mystery of Edwin Drood* Dickens powerfully conveys the effects of opium. The novel opens as a man emerges from his opiate reverie astounded by the sight of an ancient English Cathedral Tower – 'How can that be here!' – and then of a spike of rusty iron – 'Who has set it up? Maybe it is set up by the Sultan's orders for the impaling of a horde of Turkish robbers, one by one. It is so, for cymbals clash, and the Sultan goes to his palace in long procession.'

Gradually the fever settles. The objects become distinct – 'Stay! Is the spike so low a thing as the rusty spike on the top of a post of an old bedstead that has tumbled all awry? Some vague period of drowsy laughter must be devoted to the consideration of this possibility.'

And so, 'Shaking from head to foot, the man whose scattered consciousness has thus fantastically pieced itself together, at length rises, supports his trembling frame upon his arms, and looks around.'

As so often with Dickens, the opening to his book has the power of a climax, additionally so as he wrote from personal experience.

The man finds himself in the meanest and closest of small rooms, with the early light stealing in through a ragged window-curtain: 'he lies, dressed, across a large unseemly bed, upon a bedstead that has indeed given way under the weight upon it. Lying, also dressed and also across the bed, not longwise, are a Chinaman, a Lascar and a haggard woman. The two first are in a sleep or stupor; the last is blowing at a kind of pipe to kindle it.'

The woman, who has 'opium-smoked herself into a strange likeness of the Chinaman', offers him another pipe, complaining that business is slack with few Chinamen about, fewer Lascars, and no ships coming in. '"Here's another ready for ye, deary. Ye'll remember like a good soul, won't ye, that the market price is dreffle high just now? More nor three shillins and sixpence for a thimbleful! And ye'll remember that nobody but me (and Jack Chinaman t'other side the court; but he can't do it as well as me) has the true secret of mixing it? Ye'll pay up accordingly, deary, won't ye?" She blows at the pipe as she speaks, and, occasionally, bubbling at it, inhales much of its contents.'

Presumably Dickens visited such a 'den' when he stayed at Limehouse, possibly in my own house as Mr Woodward Fisher claimed, though this competed with other claims along the waterfront.

Dorian Gray, too, sought refuge in Limehouse in order 'To cure the soul by means of the senses, and the senses by means of the soul.' I assume this is the ultimate blessing for the opium smoker, though I am not too sure what it means. Dorian had no doubts: 'Yes, that was the secret. He had often tried it, and would try it again now. There were opium-dens, where one could buy oblivion, dens of horror where the memory of old sins could be destroyed by the madness of sins that were new.'

Steam rose from the horse as his hansom cab headed to Limehouse, and its windows clogged with a grey-flannel mist: 'Suddenly the man drew up with a jerk at the top of a dark lane. Over the low roofs and jagged chimney stacks of the houses rose the black masts of ships. Wreaths of white mist clung like ghostly sails to the yards.'

Finally, Dorian Gray entered

> a long, low room which looked as if it had once been a third-rate dancing saloon. Shrill flaring gas jets, dulled and distorted in the fly-blown mirrors that faced them, were ranged round the walls . . .
>
> Some Malays were crouching by a little charcoal stove playing with bone counters . . .
>
> Dorian winced, and looked round at the grotesque things that lay in such fantastic postures on the ragged mattresses. The twisted limbs, the gaping mouths, the staring lustreless eyes, fascinated him. He knew in what strange heavens they were suffering, and what dull hells were teaching them the secret of some new joy. They were better off than he was.

The descriptions by Dickens and Wilde are fiction, even if they are based on personal experience in Limehouse. Blanchard Jerrold's true account in *London – A Pilgrimage* is the most revealing. Protected by their police escort, Jerrold describes how they plunged

> into a maze of courts and narrow streets of low houses – nearly all the doors of which are open, showing kitchen fires blazing far into the interior, and strange figures moving about. Whistles, shouts, oaths, growls, and the brazen laughter of tipsy women: sullen 'good nights' to the police escort; frequent recognition of notorious rogues by the superintendent and his men; black pools of water under our feet – only a riband of violet grey sky overhead!

They continue their dark journey, from 'thieves' kitchen to lodging house –

> picking up some fresh scrap of the history of Poverty and Crime – they must go hand in hand hereabouts – at every turn.
>
> . . . the police smile when we wonder what would become of a lonely wanderer who should find himself in these regions unprotected. 'He would be stripped to his shirt.'

Finally they reach their destination: 'the dreadful paved court, flanked with tumble-down one storied houses, in which our old friend the Lascar opium smoker rolled upon his mattress, stirring his stifling narcotic over a lamp, and keeping his eyes – bright as burning coals – upon his latch.'

The inner room is familiar, described as 'the room in which *Edwin Drood* opens'. Gustave Doré's engraving, above, accompanying the description, is entitled: *Opium Smoking – The Lascar's Room in 'Edwin Drood'*. The illustration in the novel is closer to Dickens' description, but Doré's is the more haunting with the luminous figure on the bed, whose sinuous smile is lit by a small flame which fuels the elongated pipe. The sex of the creature is indeterminate.

> Upon the wreck of a four-post bedstead (the posts of which almost met overhead, and from which depended bundles of shapeless rags), upon a mattress heaped with indescribable clothes, lay, sprawling, a Lascar, dead-drunk with opium; and at the foot of the bed a woman, with a little brass lamp among the rags covering her, stirring the opium over the tiny flame.

Escaping from the opium fumes, they enter a large room with a piano and a stage:

> The entire audience turned towards us faces – the combined effect of which I shall never forget. The music stopped, and amid a general flutter our Scotland Yard sergeant, backed by the superintendent, passed the awful array of criminal countenances in steady review. We were then invited – and we needed no second invitation – to pass out. 'Not there,' said the sergeant. 'It would have been a tough job.'

The toffs continue to 'slum' – peeping at rows of sleeping vagrants – and return home 'by the flaring lights of Shadwell, looking in at the sailors' hops in Ratcliff Highway, and carrying off the honour of having been introduced to the strongest woman in Bermondsey; who was pleased to ask, in her condescending way, whether we were good for a pint of gin.'

Jerrold had the grace to admit:

> We were to them as strange and amusing as Chinamen: and we were something more and worse. We were spies upon them; men of better luck whom they were bound to envy, and whose mere presence roused the rebel in them. A few of them, loitering about the Whitechapel Road, flung a parting sneer or oath at us, as we hailed a returning cab ... It was two in the morning when we got clear of the East.

Surprisingly, a different impression of the Limehouse opium den was given by Sir Walter Besant, hardly known for his flippancy. 'Expecting a creeping of the flesh' on his first visit, he was greatly disappointed to find that 'the place was neither dreadful nor horrible.'

Besant visited a room which also sounds familiar with a great bed covered by a mattress and two men lying on it – 'enjoying the opium sleep, perhaps with the dreams that De Quincey has described' – but he views the 'horror' more objectively. A third man was smoking and half a dozen more waited for their turn, but apart from the general smell the aspect that alarmed Besant more than the rest was a musical instrument, played as if a thousand fingernails were scratching the window.

It was this, rather than the degradation of the opium smokers, which left the lingering impression: 'Nor can I understand why, under the weird and wonderful torture of the intolerable music of that instrument, even the sleepers themselves did not awake, their dreams dissipated, their opium, so to speak, wasted and rendered of none account, and fly, shrieking, forswearing forever opium and the Chinese quarter.'

Besant seems to have viewed the opium den in the clearer light of day; the others in the pitch of night when imaginations are released. Conceivably,

Besant was more accurate in making the opium dens – rather than their effect – appear unromantic.

The opium, brought from the Chinese poppyfields by Lascar and Chinese seamen, gave Limehouse an added spice of danger. Usually the dealings were conducted in darkest privacy, but an elderly woman I spoke to, daughter of a policeman in Limehouse at the time, remembered a Chinaman being chased down the street by two other Chinese. Her father and another policeman chased them in their turn and when they caught up with them found they had iron bars in their sleeves and were plainly intent on battering the other Chinese man to death who belonged to the Tong and had given offence to a rival secret society. He was so grateful to the police for saving his life that he sent £5 to the Commissioner asking if this could be shared. 'As Dad's wages was twenty-five shillings a week,' the old lady told me, 'he would have been happy to do that every day.'

After the incident, in a nearby garden, she found a counter which she still possessed. 'It's a piece of ebony, I think, with bits of ivory let in on either side which lift up. Each bit is inlaid with an insect most beautifully done. I thought it must have been thrown there by the Chinaman, and must have had some importance if he did not wish it found in his possession.'

Gradually the Chinese population decreased, between the two World Wars. One reason was a new law making it illegal to sign on a Chinese crew in any British port, which caused a drop in the number of 'celestial' sailors who had kept themselves available before.

By now Chinatown was reduced to peeling façades and memories

Opium gave way to harder drugs, for 'dope' was fashionable among the Bright Young Things in the 1930s who found the idea adventurous and headed for Limehouse in search of thrills. The sensational death of a favourite Gaiety Girl at Brilliant Chang's around the corner from the West India Docks resulted in a narcotics raid by Scotland Yard, and though Chang escaped to China, where he lost his fortune and went blind, hundreds of other Chinese were deported. By the time I arrived less than two hundred remained.

The 'slumming' had continued, with elegant young men in dinner jackets and society lovelies in clinging white gowns mixing 'dangerously' with the riff-raff as the toffs had done before them with their police escorts. The louche atmosphere was captured hilariously in an early film *The Mysterious Mr Moto* starring Peter Lorre which showed a Limehouse pub where French sailors danced with fat ladies to the accordion, and villains fought each other while a man died from poison in a corner. 'My!' exclaimed one of the West End beauties, 'what *lovely local colour*!'

There was one pub when I arrived which actually fulfilled this image in reality: Charley Brown's near the gates of West India Docks, underneath the arches which upheld the trains as they rattled towards the City. More prosaically, and accurately, the pub was called the Railway Tavern, but everyone knew it as Charley Brown's, after the landlord. He had acquired a legendary collection of macabre souvenirs, added to by sailors when they returned from distant and exotic places: a two-headed calf; a mummy that was half fish and half baby; numerous assegai and poisoned arrows; African masks; carved teak from the East; and various nasty things in bottles.

My father told me of this, and his visits to Charley Brown's in the thirties which included an incident that might have come from *Limehouse Nights*, which he related in his book, *Bomber's Moon*. He was talking one night to Rosie, who was tattooed with three seagulls in graceful flight across her 'red, ham-like arm', when a girl came up and put her arms around them – one each. My father remembered Pearl as a 'popular' Limehouse girl who earned £5 a week.

'Honest,' she pleaded to Rose, 'you know I loved that man.'

'Yes,' said Rose, unimpressed, 'and what did you do to him?'

Ironically, Pearl whose eyes were swollen from weeping, was not paying for the wages of sin, but for having gone straight after falling in love with a man from Limehouse. She had worked for him instead, hard and honestly, until she discovered what nearly everybody else knew, that her man was two-timing her. Starting to embarrass Rose and my father, she poured out her troubles emotionally.

'I didn't mind getting bashed abaht a bit – we expects that; and when he came home and began to slosh me that night I took it. But he was so drunk he didn't know what he was *saying* . . . ! He told me her name . . . he laughed at me . . . and do you know what I did?'

'Yes, we all knows what you did,' said Rose, phlegmatically.

'I don't mean that – what I did *first?*'

'Tell this gentleman, if 'e cares to listen.'

For a moment Pearl cheered up as she recollected her revenge: 'I waited until he was in a snooze, and then I took all his clothes off him. I went out on the landing and sung out: "Girls! Do you want to have a ripping time?" And when they come I told them to go back and bring their scissors. And do you know what we did then? We cut up all his clothes into *teeny-weeny* little bits ...' she measured with a finger nail to show just how teeny they were ...

Rosie snorted with disgust: 'And *then* what did you do? You *informed* on 'im – that's wot. And you got your man sent up for five years for arson, didn't yer?'

In the ensuing tears, Pearl sobbed as she assured her friend: 'I've been rehearsing every night what I'm going to say to that man when he gets out.'

'Oh, shove off!' said Rosie, jerking her shoulder loose. 'You 'op it! Me and this gentleman wants to talk together.'

After Pearl had gone, Rosie turned to my father sarcastically: 'Rehearsing what she's going to say to him when he gets out! Not 'arf she will!'

'Why not?' asked my father.

'Because she'll never set eyes on that man again. Soon's his time's up, they put him straight back on board a ship, send 'im home.'

'Why?'

''Cause he's a Chink.'

Yet the Police Court Missionary had told my father that 'John Chinaman' (such condescension!) usually made the best husband on earth because he was so faithful. Also, that there was no point in expecting him to swear on the Bible in court:

> That, to him, was just one of life's great jokes. No; you must make him swear the Saucer or the Candle Oath. Make him take a saucer and say, 'If I tell a lie, may my soul be shattered into a thousand pieces – *like that!*' Then he would slam the saucer on the stone floor, pieces flying all over the place. Or, with the candle: 'If I tell a lie, may my soul be blown out – *like that!*' Pouf – and he would blow out the candle.

The Police Court Missionary stressed that when he took an oath like that, the Chinaman was scrupulous in giving evidence – *'You must bind him by his own code.'*

Returning to Limehouse in the Blitz, my father noticed a solitary Chinaman running down Limehouse Causeway when the 'Alert' siren sounded, and found it prophetic. 'For there in the flesh, went a remnant of the old London which is passing. With it were going types: the crews of ships, a certain kind of white girl, and a literature. I'm not sure that London won't lose by it.'

In spite of the opium dens and internecine Tong, the Chinese contributed their colourful piece to the general jig-saw of the East End. A docker told me that his life was centred round Limehouse until his twenties, as one of twelve children,

> born in Northy Street around the corner where you live now, educated in that wonderful school, the Cyril Jackson, sitting side by side with Chinese and half-castes and thinking nothing about it other than how clever they invariably were, how softly spoken and polite.
>
> My dad worked in Dundee Wharf in those days and used to bring home his gambling pukka-poo papers for us to help fill in, small sheets with Chinese characters on them. How my mother cursed them! We used to visit with our Chinese friends to their homes, usually above a restaurant with exotic smells and peculiar images in the windows. As children we accepted them just as they accepted us.

There was little more than an echo of this happily enclosed community when I arrived, but one legendary Limehouse landmark remained. Around the corner from Narrow Street, less than five minutes' walk from my home, Charley Brown's was still there. Charley himself had moved on to the great public house in the sky (or more likely to a garden suburb to retire on his profits). The souvenirs had gone with him, apart from a few dust-covered relics of little interest; and the pianola had been replaced by a jukebox. Perhaps it was even seedier than before, resembling a dimly lit cavern with its curved ceiling, and I loved it on sight. Lascars still scurried past outside, on a sortie from the West India Docks, and merchant seamen half-filled the place at night, shouting at each other in their various tongues. This was a waterfront pub exemplified by *The Mysterious Mr Moto*, complete with arguments and fisticuffs. Surprisingly, the violence came from the upright landlord – a military-looking man – and his wife, dark-haired and too attractive for her own or anybody else's good. Throughout the day I looked forward to entering Charley Brown's in the evening to learn the latest fracas. Once a policeman stopped me as I reached the door. 'Bad one this time,' he warned me, shaking his head. 'He's charging her with being on the game. I'm off to arrest her in the Opporto.'

'Surely not!' I replied. 'I'm sure he doesn't mean it.'

'He's lodged an official complaint, hasn't he?'

'Has he?'

Another time, he tried to kill her by breaking a bottle over her head. He missed but left a nasty crevice in the bar.

Returning the next morning to see if she was alive, I found the landlord, his clipped, greying moustache as moist from champagne as his eyes were tearful with remorse behind his specs. 'The friendly enemy', as he called her, was immaculately made-up and coiffed as always and greeted me with a pealing laugh as he opened another bottle and toasted her health. Her make-up was particularly thick under her right eye, but reconciliation was a very heaven and the threatened violence just a game and rarely realised. This was not the view of the scandalised brewers, always narrow-minded, who were so alarmed by the police reports that the couple were moved to another pub in the more salubrious air of Croydon. I went to see them there but the outward respectability which made them so welcome at first had slipped already, and they were on the move again. They had suited the eccentric waterfront atmosphere of Limehouse so well, their prim façade concealing a seething undercurrent of passion.

10

The two Miss Littlewoods

As I SETTLED into Narrow Street, I met the families in the 'Buildings' opposite. Once they realised that I loved the place, they absolved me from 'slumming' and I was accepted, by the children in particular. Though Limehouse lined the Thames, there were surprisingly few places where the river could be seen, and the local children watched it from my balcony, entranced.

I have never been good with children, trying to speak to them in their language instead of my own, but these – bright, inquisitive, humorous and self-confident – made me feel at ease. One little girl, with long ringlets and a roguish finger thrust into the corner of her mouth, was a potential beauty – and knew it. An older boy, inclined to be cheeky and show-off, was a potential bully, but he was at the turning point of growing-up, so beset by problems that at times his eyes were anguished, like someone who stammers, searching for the right words. Possibly he had difficulties at home, but he seemed at ease at Narrow Street and quietened down.

I was an oddity to them, surrounded by piles of books and a confusion of papers, alien to the pristine tidiness of the East End.

My pictures baffled them, especially a worthless print of Adam and Eve bought in the alleys of Marrakesh.

'Wassat?'

'That's Adam and Eve.'

'oo they?'

'The first man and woman in the world.'

'Cor!' followed by a cry to the others: 'Come and look at Dan's dirty picture.' Adam and Eve were covered discreetly, but I dreaded their explanation when they returned to their families – 'And what have you been up to?' 'Looking at Dan's dirty pictures, 'aven't we.'

Any doubts that I might have had about the children wandering around my home would have been resolved by my housekeeper, Rose.

Meeting her was the best luck I had in all my years in the East End: constantly cheerful, she coped with my chaos uncomplainingly, in spite of a brief scowl of dismay as she saw the debris of the morning after. ''ad another bleedin' party, Dan?' she'd say, without reproach. Rose was the personification of cockney wit and loyalty and I was blessed to know her. She was popular with my friends and made them welcome. Her husband, Bob, called her 'Blossom' and the nickname suited her for she possessed the full-blown radiance of many cockney women, with a rosiness of her own.

Saints should have their drawbacks: Rose's, at that time, was her son, now an upright young man, then a devil as he stomped around Narrow Street with an imitation hand-gun, smashing the ancient, encrusted amphora on the balcony which I had brought from Greece, banging holes in the early Italian marble slab which I had bought in a smart antique shop in Pimlico, and which served as a table, the most valuable object I possessed though considerably less so after the ravages of that particular day.

How could I complain when she never complained herself? It was Bob who insisted, wisely, that the insane Fritz (Ted the minder's dog) be locked up while she was there, otherwise she accepted him as another hazard.

It was Rose who allowed the local children in and kept an eye on them.

In their turn, they proved helpful (as I shall explain) when Joan Littlewood asked me to become the 'Adviser to the Director' on her forthcoming film, *Sparrers Can't Sing*. My title was greeted with laughter by those who knew her, for Joan did not need advice; indeed she regarded advice as unwelcome, and was the last person to take it.

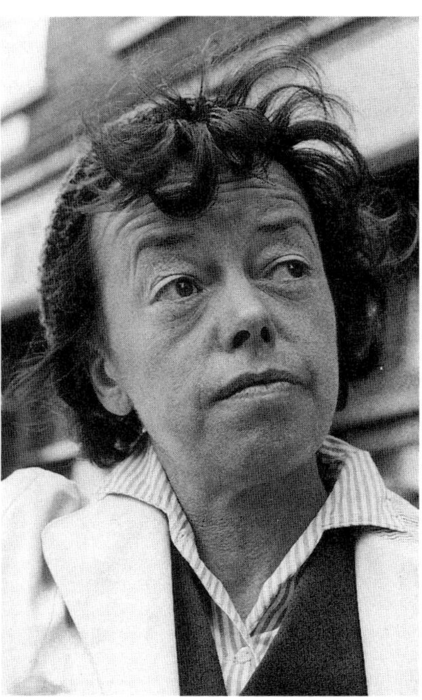

Joan Littlewood directing Sparrers.

I suspect that she asked me on impulse when we met in the Colony Room in Soho and she heard that I was living in Limehouse. I was delighted, though I did not appreciate that Joan was a legendary figure in the theatre, and I was I scarcely aware of the Theatre Royal at Stratford East which she ran in partnership with Gerry Raffles. Later I realised its importance as the only surviving theatre in the East End, apart from the Yiddish Theatre in Commercial Road. The Pavilion was now derelict – I had photographed the ruins one morning, and few sights are so forlorn as a gutted theatre – and the old Music Halls were either closed or had vanished without trace. The Theatre Royal is still one of the loveliest theatres in London, and there is little doubt that it would have been closed without the persistence of Joan Littlewood and Gerry Raffles who loved it as if it had been their child.

Sparrers, by Stephen Lewis, had been staged at the Theatre Royal and seemed a natural choice for her first film, fulfilling her desire for cockney capers: outside lavatories, tarts with hearts of gold, lovely villains and cheerful bar-room brawls.

Though I dared not express such heresy aloud, I had the uneasy suspicion that Joan's concept of the East End was not only condescending but inaccurate. I have mentioned her transformation of the Kentucky Club's gentility into something sleezy yet high-spirited. In the film she reduced the East End to a cliché of punch-ups and knees-ups, avoiding the harsh reality of such northern films as *Saturday Night, Sunday Morning*.

This dreadful thought was confirmed when I spoke to a stallholder in the Stratford market near the theatre, where black eels slithered in wooden boxes and the atmosphere actually fulfilled her fantasy.

The stallholder, who was highly educated, was giving me his views on Marcel Proust when he broke off suddenly with a flurry of obscene gestures and shouts of 'Up yours!', followed by 'good on yer gal,' and I looked round to see Joan scurrying past with similar shadow-boxing gestures of her own.

'Please forgive me,' he continued in his impeccable accent after she had gone, 'but Joan *does* like us to talk like that.'

As I write this I feel guilty of betrayal. Joan had a touch of genius, a whirlwind of a woman, and the territory she crossed was never quite the same again.

She threw herself into the film with astounding energy, rewriting the semblance of a script into the early hours, often having no sleep at all. Throughout her life, if she has failed to spare other people, she has never spared herself.

Since she was new to filming, every day was a battle, especially with the cameraman, a veteran of the old school who took an eternity in 'setting-up', though Joan's strength lay in her spontaneity, on which the film depended. 'The bastard's used to lighting Anna Neagle,' she muttered to me as he gazed through his view-finder, and at one point she threatened to remove her name from the production. The technicians admired her, never having seen a director work so hard before, but it became clear that either she would have to adapt to the red-tape and the rules of the industry, or the industry to her. She won, but I have never heard of people arriving on a film set and leaving it so quickly.

A small, untidy, ageless figure in a dirty white mackintosh and red-knitted cap, she established an absolute control, partly due to her ability to stare someone directly in the face with an expression which implied, 'You are the one person I need at this moment, and you know it.'

During the filming I happened to go to a party one evening where several actors who had worked with her vied with stories of the horrible things she had done to them: her charm, abandoned so swiftly once they had served their purpose; her interference in their private lives; her cruelty in pursuit of her own perfection which approached a state of chaos. Then there was the hypocrisy of her champagne socialism and her move to a penthouse in the Dorchester when she tired of the elegant house in Blackheath which she shared with Gerry Raffles.

As the pent-up grievances poured out, a monstrous image emerged, genie-like, until one of the actors, Alfred Lynch, started to laugh. 'And do you know,' he told us, 'after all the terrible things we've said, if I received a cable from Joan tomorrow telling me she needed me in Nigeria for the next six months, *without* pay, I'd take the next plane.' And all the rest agreed.

Sparrers started with a merchant seaman coming home on leave, and Joan as she was wont to do, sprang a surprise one evening when she told me I was playing a ship's officer and would be handed my Equity card in the morning.

Like many people I indulge in the fantasy of appearing on stage to tumultuous applause, and actually have a recurring dream in which I am asked to take over at the last moment and do so, even though I do not know my lines. At least my dream rebukes such vanity with the threat of incipient disaster before I wake. Now Joan had given me my chance, as she had done for Michael Caine and many others. Knowing her relish for vitality, I considered coming on like Captain Bligh until I discovered that my few lines hardly justified bravura, just 'Have a good time on shore', 'Don't do anything I wouldn't do', 'Remember we sail in a week's time', or something equally mundane. As her adviser, I sought advice desperately on how I should pitch my performance, but she was too preoccupied. When my moment arrived, I spoke my lines with a winning smile, more in the manner of Cary Grant than Laughton. When they were over no one made any comment until her brief and cold announcement that 'the scene didn't work. We've cut it'.

The filming had taken place on board a ship in the West India Docks and we were invited to join a cocktail party that the shipping line were holding the following night. It was a rash invitation, for the ship's officer expected a couple of the senior members of the film unit to attend in evening dress: possibly the producer, and of course Joan Littlewood herself. He did not expect the typical entourage of Littlewood 'clowns' including an actor who was acting as if he was drugged, as indeed he was; two huge 'villains' whom Joan employed as bodyguards for the unit, and various stragglers – dockers, seamen and tarts who attached themselves to Joan during the day. The outraged steward closed the bar and Joan was the only member of the film crew to be offered a canape, along with the ship's officers and their wives. A nasty scene was averted as her own crew left rapidly, with many an insult hurled.

The next morning Joan summoned one of her assistants. 'This must *never* happen again,' she told him.

'It's all right,' he assured her. 'I heard what happened and apologised for all of you.'

'What I meant,' she replied furiously, 'was that in future when I'm invited, *everyone*'s invited. Got that?' She never forgave him.

The filming was fun. Unlike many, I did not object to the interminable hanging-about on the film set, and with Joan there was the added interest of filming on location with real places and real people. Her haphazard approach to filming dismayed the producer, who tried to lure her back to the studio where he could keep her under control, but Joan regarded *Sparrers* as an 'adventure', imploring her actors to 'enjoy it a bit more'. When a scene went badly, she told them: 'Don't do it *again*. Think it's the first time and enjoy yourself. Make up different words if you want to.'

Failing to appreciate my luck in working with someone so special, I did not cultivate the opportunity as I should have done, refusing a last-minute invitation from Gerry Raffles to join them for the weekend on his boat at Portsmouth. The trouble was that no one ever explained anything. I had no idea of her relationship with Raffles, though she spoke to him so abusively that I assumed they were in love, nor had I any knowledge of a boat. Why had they asked me? Who would be there? What did they want of me? Far from acting from vanity, my reluctance to join in was a misjudged modesty. I had the suspicion that I would be on trial, an initiation before I was accepted as one of her 'nuts', and I was not sure if I was ready to offer myself as a sacrifice.

I went to the party she held in the flat she rented in Cable Street after she was asked to leave the elegant Old Vicarage at the end of my street. It was such a good party that she was asked to leave Cable Street as well, after the people underneath complained about the ceiling, most of which had fallen in. That was when, as far as I remember, she moved to the Dorchester.

My role became that of a Limehouse runner, sometimes receiving messages at midnight. These might be cries for help – 'This film is the most nightmarish business of my entire life' – but usually they were demands: 'Six tough merchant seamen needed for a punch-up in the strip-tease scene, by midday' or 'Four tarts by lunchtime'.

Barbara Windsor waiting for her call in a common street

For the former, with an audacity which amazes me today, I hurried to Charley Brown's at opening time and accosted a group of massive Scandinavian seamen who followed me with the docility of sheep. The 'prostitutes', or 'ladies of ill-fame' as Joan described them archaically, presented more of a problem, which I solved by asking the most glamorous wives of my East End friends if they would like to appear in a film. 'If so, would they wear their very best clothes – you know,' giving a carefree laugh, 'something nice and tarty.' Then I hurried to the Eastern Hotel at Gardiner's corner to enlist the help of the one-eyed lady with scarlet hair who screeched out 'I ain't got nobody' to the wail of a silver trumpet and a banjo on Friday nights. All of them arrived on time, Joan approved of their appearance and told them what to do, and everyone was happy with little idea of their casting.

Joan had the flair to treat the local villains as aristocracy, and she spoke to the children as if they were adults. I cast them from the Buildings opposite and could see that she was startled by their sophistication. At one point she turned on me unpleasantly: 'These children are far too *cynical* to be in my film.' Or too professional? I think she was expecting urchins.

One warm spring afternoon, when the filming was drawing to its close, I walked back to Narrow Street – an approach which always gave me pleasure, with the great black anchor on the warehouse wall ahead – and found a boy sitting on my doorstep.

'Seen yer pup?' he asked.

'I don't have one.'

'Yer do now.'

I went upstairs to find the 'Limehouse Terrors', as Joan had called them, on their hands and knees, peering at something underneath the sofa.

For once they looked at me nervously. Heading for the kitchen, I found that even Rose looked discomfited. 'I didn't know what to do for the best,' she protested before I could speak. 'One of the boys bought her in the market on Sunday and of course his father won't allow him to keep a pup in the Buildings, so he's brought her here.'

'For me to look after?'

'Didn't have the heart to turn them away,' she replied, lamely.

My good humour gone, I returned to the living-room to be handed a small bunch of damp, black fur. The puppy could not have been more than a few weeks old and the boys and I looked at her helplessly. Saucers of water and scraps of food surrounded the sofa in the hope of enticing her, but she had not touched them.

'What am I supposed to do?'

'We heard you wanted a dog.'

'Yes, but a *guard* dog. An Alsatian or something, not *this*.' We studied the bedraggled object which looked half dead.

'You see,' said the boy who owned her, 'my Dad says she'll have to be put down ...' He dared not finish the sentence nor look me in the face, though other pairs of eyes watched me intently. The silence was taut as I realised I was trapped. Stretching his luck, the boy continued, 'Her name is Trixie – Trix.'

'Oh no it isn't,' I exclaimed to sighs of relief as they realised I was beaten. 'I'll call her ...' I searched for a name and found one near at hand '... *Littlewood*!'

'That's not a *dog*'s name.' The chorus was scornful, but Rose emerged from the kitchen drying her hands, pleased that the matter had been settled. 'Littlewood,' she explained cheerfully, 'after the Pools. And I bet there'll be plenty of them to clean up afterwards.'

Returning home late that night, I had almost forgotten the dog, even assuming that such an inanimate object would be dead by morning. Instead, Littlewood flew across the room and smothered me with kisses. Racing wildly around me she had come back to life with a vengeance, and I sat down on the sofa struggling with Littlewood's ecstasy and my own laughter – as I continued to do for the next twelve fortunate years.

She developed rapidly, though she was scrawny at first. Later Tom Driberg described her in his Sunday column as 'a beautiful, spaniel-type mongrel bitch' and so she became after losing her early gawkiness. To Littlewood the East End had been put there at her disposal; it never occurred to her someone might dislike her. Few people did, though I noticed that Joan looked askance when I told Littlewood to behave herself, forgetting that I had called the dog after her. Far from being flattered, when I tried to explain, Joan was unamused.

Her diet was peculiar: she favoured raw eggs, liver, snow and chicken Chow Mein. After someone foolishly put beer in her water bowl, Littlewood insisted on running water from the tap. Once she varied her diet by tearing a book of poems, given me by Gregory Corso after he came to Narrow Street, into small pieces which she devoured before I could stop her. Another time I saw her remove a slim volume from the bookshelf in her mouth, a feat achieved with considerable care until I rescued it.

Littlewood knew no danger, no enemy and no fear, which proved a liability. Following anyone she took a liking to, she escaped on several occasions while I searched for her frantically, cursing every lorry which charged along the road. Once two friendly dockers brought her back, having recognised her as she headed towards the West India Docks. Another time I was told to fetch her from the police station where she was tethered by a chain, each link as big as herself, ample enough to secure a lion. The police were immune to her charm, though she was unconcerned.

As I have mentioned, she alone could intimidate the insane Doberman called Fritz during his short-lived reign of terror when he arrived with Ted the minder at Narrow Street. Another encounter with a dog took place at a children's party where she was exiled to a separate room because of her high spirits, joining another dog who took an immediate interest as she danced around him wildly.

A few minutes later a man burst into the room and cried out in horror, 'Get that *thing* out of here.'

Hearing the commotion, I arrived to find out what had happened.

'Don't you realise, he's about to go on.'

'What are you talking about?' I asked indignantly, on Littlewood's behalf.

'This isn't an ordinary dog, *this* is a performing dog and he's supposed to be remembering his numbers. Now he's so worked up that when I call out black he'll probably pick the red!'

And sure enough he did, wrecking the act of the conjuror who looked as if he wished to strangle Littlewood. The performing dog gazed at her adoringly, his heart no longer in his performance.

There were moments of near disaster, like the time she was locked outside by mistake when it was snowing and found shivering by the workmen in the street the next morning; she recovered but it took her a day before she forgave me and months before I forgave myself. Otherwise she enhanced my life. When she had a litter, I would drive the remaining puppies and herself to Greenwich Park or lead them through the tunnel underneath the river from the Isle of Dogs. Up the hill past the Royal Naval College and the Queen's House we would climb to the top of the hill until we reached the Royal Observatory which gave the world 'Greenwich Mean Time'. Such explorations introduced me to areas which might have evaded me otherwise, with Littlewood as the joyful justification.

However, I should remember that other people's dogs are as boring as other people's babies, dreams and gardens, and I shall resist writing about her further. As I do so now, her great grand-daughter, the last of the line, is beside me, approaching the age of sixteen: a lovely old dog with much of the same courageous spirit as the puppy brought to me at Limehouse.

When *Sparrers* was eventually completed, Joan Littlewood dismissed it to Ken Tynan as 'a primitive thing', yet in many ways it was neither primitive nor outrageous enough. It requires considerable discipline to appear so undisciplined.

A few years later I worked with her again, more closely and traumatically. She had reached a trough after a series of giddy successes, starting with *A Taste of Honey* by Shelagh Delaney, followed by *Fings Ain't Wot They Used T'Be*, by Frank Norman; *The Hostage* by Brendan Behan; and *Oh, What a Lovely War!* Yet it needed money to keep the Theatre Royal going and by now she had been forced to compromise by leasing it out, producing her own shows in the upstairs room of the pub opposite. As she led me around the empty theatre, now painted in psychedelic colours, she pointed to white prints on the pavement which led to the pub. 'That's our tiger,' she explained. Above us stretched some bunting which should have spelled 'MUSIC HALL' except that some of the letters had fallen off. Considering that Joan Littlewood was one of the most innovative figures of the British Theatre in this century, it was shocking.

For the next few months we worked together on a musical about Marie Lloyd which I had written with the late Harry Moore, providing lyrics for the new music by Norman Kaye though I began to realise that it was impossible to compete with the familiarity of Marie's own songs like 'My Old Man'.

Joan and Gerry were so stretched that I raised half the production money by enlisting friends as 'angels' prepared to back the show. It disturbed me when someone asked 'Why on earth didn't you go ahead and produce it on your own?' for the idea had never occurred to me, because I was new to the game and trusted Joan implicitly.

Attending the first rehearsal – a daunting moment which any writer would savour – I was surprised by the actors doing strange things, like dragging a grown woman across the stage who was howling like a baby. I smiled amiably, assuming that this was a scene from another, somewhat surrealist production, until I realised this was *Marie*. Not a word of my dialogue remained. No one had prepared me that this was the way that Joan worked, though I should have guessed after *Sparrers*. Yet again, no one had explained.

On the third day she beckoned me to join her on the stage where she glowered at me through her hooded eyes and half-spectacles with their metal frames.

'It's no good. I can't go through with it. It's not going to work. I'm miserable, you're miserable.'

My throat was dry. 'But Joan, I couldn't be happier. I agree with everything you've suggested,' even though this was far from the truth.

'I can't work this way. I'm an egomaniac, no, I'm not, it's just that I'm too old. I don't care if I break people's hearts. This is the only way I can work.' She mentioned that she had broken Frank Norman and Brendan Behan and, for a fatuous moment, I felt elation at being in their company. She continued harshly in a whisper: 'I don't think you know a thing about the theatre. I don't believe you can write dialogue [she was not too sure of Shakespeare either: 'Bill wasn't a bad old hack but we don't respect him']. Norman comes here and has the audacity to tell me what to do; Harry sits there looking like death and upsets the actors ... I can only work my way. I thought you understood that.'

The words spattered out venomously, yet anyone watching might have thought we were having a friendly chat, and Norman sat there in the stalls beaming.

'And you're too concerned.'

'Wouldn't it be awful if I wasn't?' I managed to say, with a glazed smile.

'I mean it. I'm dead serious.' She gave me a cold look and walked away. We were barred from the theatre.

Of course she was right. Our constant presence was intolerable, apart from Norman's who needed to guide her through the score. It would have been so much better to give her a few pages of script and hope for the best. We cared too much.

Gerry tried to console me: 'You'll be surprised how much remains when you see it.'

Ultimately, it was a close-run thing. Joan's flaw was an inability to change a scene when it failed to work; instead of scrapping it, she turned it upside down. There was the perennial challenge – who could convey Marie's magic? –

but Avis Bunnage rose to the occasion, and the costumes by the late Pearl Binder had the right period flavour. Joan showed touches of her theatrical genius, and impeccable taste in her recreation of a Music Hall.

The playwright, Frank Marcus, author of *The Killing of Sister George*, voted it the best musical of the year in the annual London Critics' poll conducted by *Variety*, and the transfer looked so certain that I wandered around in a state of author's euphoria.

And then our time ran out. The theatre had been leased to another company on Boxing Day, and the impresario – I think he was Donald Alberry – changed his mind about the transfer to a West End theatre at the last moment. Lifelines were sought, but, like the relief of General Gordon, too late, too late.

On the last night, Christmas Eve 1967, I phoned Joan and Gerry suggesting a farewell drink and we met in an Aldgate pub, crowded with colourful cockney characters as if in parody of *Sparrers*. No longer the ring-master with the shadow-boxing gestures and those sinister half specs, Joan looked radiant. She wore a dustman's jacket embroidered with the red-lettering 'Borough of Hackney' but instead of her usual woolly cap she wore an elegant hat made of mink which some local children had given her after she spoke up for them in the magistrate's court earlier that week.

'Nicked it!' she said proudly.

Today she lives in France, where Gerry Raffles died suddenly in 1977. The area outside the Theatre Royal has been re-named Gerry Raffles Square in their honour.

11

Pursuits of Happiness

THE EAST ENDERS enjoyed a keen sense of family unity, with the mother in the dominant role, in direct contrast to the West End where father ruled the roost and his wife obeyed. Up West you hardly knew your neighbour, yet friends and neighbours were an essential part of East End life, and the sympathy of pubs another. At closing time it was commonplace to carry the upright piano across the street into someone's house in order to prolong the sing-song. The lyrics of these songs testify to the comradeship: 'Dear Old Pals' (originally pals in the army) and 'Call round any old time and make yourself at home – rich or poor – knock at the door – and make yourself at home'.

Parties were a vital distraction, with the women seated in lines against the wall, and East Enders borrowed each other's clothes to go dancing: 'It was like a village life, we didn't go outside our territory.'

Life in the East End moved for so many along limited lines: simplified, it was marriage and family for the girl, sport or crime for the boy. But even if theirs was a lifetime of drudgery, the spirit of the East Enders was such that – just as the tradition of Music Hall had proved that their lives were not 'unadorned by grace or splendour' – they had various pursuits of happiness in which to seek relief.

Boxing

Sport meant boxing which meant promise. There was the famous Repton Boys Club in Cheshire Street, subsidised by the English Public School, with a ring to keep the local boys from mischief; the Devonshire in Hackney; even the Double R offered the chance to better oneself. Boxing was a form of release, with an opportunity to gain respect. For the Krays it proved inadequate, though they turned it to use as a means of intimidation, but merely the fact that they were boxers enhanced their image as local heroes, in the tradition of Pedlar Palmer from Canning Town, who won the bantam-weight title in 1895, and the later heroes 'Kid' Lewis from Stepney, and 'Kid' Berg, the Whitechapel Whirlwind, who won the light welter-weight championship and held it when he went to America.

Once in the East End, I was attracted to the ring and joined my friends at local contests at places like the West Ham Baths. Boxing has no élite: it belongs to the crowd. When I was invited to the Sporting Club at the Café Royal as the guest of Charles Forte, whom I was interviewing for television at the time, I was slightly repelled by the contrast between the fat-cat tycoons replete in their dinner jackets, a bowl of brandy in one pudgy hand and long cigar in the other, and the two young men who slogged it out in the ring, with applause at the end of the round though none during it, according to club rules.

By comparison, I relished the matches I went to now: the general razzmatazz, the smoke, the warm exchanges of the East Enders dressed up for the occasion as they greeted each other in the numerous bars, the announcement by the master of ceremonies as a celebrity like George Raft climbed into the ring, the dimming of the lights for the main contest and the fanfares as the top contenders forged their way with a flurry of elbows towards prosperity or back to obscurity.

Once when I had met David Frost at a grander fight at Wembley, escorting his girlfriend Janette Scott, I was genuinely surprised when he admitted with a giggle that he was there in order to be seen. Perhaps my idolatry now was equally patronising, but boxers had the glamour of toreadors and I succumbed as much as any of the East Enders. I took pride in the company of Terry Spinks and Sammy McArthy and other ex-champions who ended up as landlords of a pub with their Lonsdale belts displayed with justifiable swank in a glass case behind the bar.

Others were less fortunate. It is the nature of the boxer's fame, brutish and short-lived, that he should be left with a sense of loss once it is over. For some, it could be redeemed by crime – petty in most cases, heinous in that of the Krays. The honourable exceptions were the Cooper brothers, also identical twins, whose reputation was impeccable. They trained upstairs at the Thomas-a-Becket in the Old Kent Road under the benevolent eye of Jim Wicks even though he was noted for his reminiscences of razor gangs on the race tracks.

The other exceptions were the Walker brothers. When I moved into Limehouse, Billy Walker was the local hero. Twenty-three years old, he was handsome, friendly and smiling; but it was his elder brother George who caught the attention, darker, leaner, with a vaulting ambition. An early news photograph of Georgie (as he was known), with Billy Hill and the 'double-agent' Eddie Chapman, reveals the haunted, romantic looks of a young John Garfield. These had been re-arranged in a fight that was still spoken of with awe. He laughed when I told him of the rumour that his opponent had lost three pints of blood – 'Absolutely ridiculous. A lot of blood was lost, both his and mine, but nothing like that.' He conceded that it had been a hard fight: 'Pretty bad, yes. I was physically exhausted, so was he. I remember they helped him down the steps of the ring and he collapsed at the bottom. At least I walked down on my own, so all in all I thought I was superior. But I lost the fight.'

In spite of a severe eye injury, George Walker endured two more fights, after which he had the sense to retire. This did not mean the end of his sporting career, for he switched his attention to Billy, promoting him as the Blonde Bombshell and a potential heavyweight champion noted for his right-hand punch. The press scented an idol and busily built him up romantically as an East End Hercules and Adonis; though, for once, having succeeded, they failed to knock him down, for Billy retained his gentle modesty throughout.

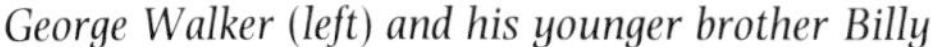

George Walker (left) and his younger brother Billy

George had left school at the age of fourteen to work as a porter in Billingsgate Fish Market. It is true that he brushed against the law when he was arrested at the age of twenty-six as he tried to drive some stolen goods through the gates of a London dockyard, but, although this was resurrected by the press a few years ago, it could be argued that his action was part of the East End love for such a man, and it is more significant that Walker was able to put the short sentence behind him and rise above it.

To start with, George Walker fulfilled himself vicariously through his brother Billy, whom he matched against John Prescott with such skill that the public was ensured their money's worth with a fighting finish. Admired for his triumph at the Olympics where he fought as an amateur and laid out his American opponent with a stunning knock-out punch, Billy had won 24 of his 33 amateur contests which were stopped within the distance, usually in the first or second rounds. George encouraged him to turn professional and when I met him he was being groomed as a challenger for Henry Cooper, and earning considerable money from various side-shoots in the process, including his 'life story' in the *News of the World*.

Billy seemed surprised by my naivety when I asked if money was the motivation for turning professional. He explained that the most he could hope for as an amateur was a five-guinea prize, compared to the £3,000 per fight he was earning now.

Though Billy proved a popular fighter, his critics said there was not enough hate in him. Naturally, George disagreed: 'If he hurts a man or gets hurt himself, that's where Billy shows himself. You know the fighter that gets hurt fights back and shows a killer instinct, and that's what Billy's got. When he's hurt he gets wicked.'

I mentioned to Billy that Henry Cooper had told me he hated his opponent so much that when he stepped into the ring he almost swore abuse at him, and Billy admitted to 'some kind of hate' but sounded decidedly gentle as he did so. He admitted his dislike of the fickle nature of the crowd who were starting to call him Puffing Billy – the inevitable nickname – and George added that 'the biggest thing that can happen for the public is to see Billy get beat now. That would be the sensation of sensations, and everybody wants sensations.'

Billy remembered his fourth fight, and his first taste of disillusionment: 'I was matched with someone much better than myself and I was decisively beaten, and it was a great shock. I put up a good fight but I was well beaten and the same crowd, my crowd, that was cheering me a few weeks before, was booing the house out. Really booing me you know, and from then on I realised that you can't rely on a boxing crowd.'

'A very hard sport,' said George, 'a very cynical crowd.'

Yet the fickleness of the crowd, hoping for blood, was part of the nature of the sport. No wonder that the boxer's motivation was money. In retrospect, the Walkers' aims were modest: 'If Billy fights well and doesn't lose any fights,' said George, 'in five years it could come to a lot of money. In three years, say, he could get £20,000.'

'If we finish up with that in the bank, we should be quite satisfied,' Billy agreed. 'Naturally I want to settle down one day, get married, and I'd like to have enough to buy a nice business that will look after me for the rest of my life, without working too hard, and not have any money worries.'

'I'll make him as rich as I possibly can by managing him,' said George.

Billy Walker did not become the heavy-weight champion, but he did well enough with George's assistance to run the Baked Potato restaurant in the old Scott's Restaurant in Leicester Square, before retiring to the Channel Isles.

As for George Walker, his story is one of the outstanding successes in the history of the East End. Expanding into other forms of 'leisure', he enjoyed a commercial scoop with such films as *The Stud*, which activated the flagging career of Joan Collins, and his own story has the cut and thrust to be celebrated on film in the future.

In 1989, as the power behind the Brent Walker Leisure Group, he paid £685 million for the betting shops of William Hill and Mecca which made him the second biggest bookmaker in the country; when his past record was brought to the attention of the Gaming Board they told him to 'forget it'. Today, he controls 1,000 public houses; Elstree Film Studio; the Lyceum Theatre off the Strand (where my great-uncle, Bram Stoker, acted as manager for Henry Irving); the Brighton Marina; and the Trocadero, as the final enhancement of his progress from the East End to the heart of London. His determination to make something of himself has been achieved beyond anything we could have envisaged then, even at the risk of overstretching himself.

A Matter of Taste

I enjoyed my few visits to George Walker's home near by, for it was different. Like all East Enders, George and his sympathetic wife were hospitable, and he was a Do-It-Yourself enthusiast, though he aimed higher than usual: he decorated an entire wall with paving stones made, as far as I can remember, of Portland stone, and the effect was impressive, even overwhelming by comparison to the usual East End decor which teetered on gentility.

Whereas my sitting-room revelled in its chaos, like a dog off the lead, an East End lounge was meticulous and highly polished, with every object firmly in its place. This pristine effect was born of necessity due to lack of space, and the house-proud neatness could have been a reaction to the surrounding slums. Marie Lloyd, for instance, was an obsessive tidier, as if an ordered house would make her own life seem in order.

The etiquette was rigid, and various objects of the East End home became familiar: the toilet-roll cover in the form of a ballerina; blue rinse inside the toilet bowl; furniture consisting of a three-piece suite in colourful Draylon; a telephone table with spring ashtray; a massive radiogram in polished veneer, with a record-holder with yellow chords containing LPs by Perry Como, Frankie Lane and Jimmy Young – and a rubber plant.

And of course there was the obligatory bar in the corner, with a round, metallic-blue ice-bucket on the counter, bottles of Snowball behind, and various signs and insignia on the wall. Other decorations included the Green Lady and a bull-fighting poster bought on the Costa Brava with the name of the toreador replaced by that of the East Ender.

Oh yes! a fireplace with flaming artificial logs, and tongs which chimed.

How odious my snobbery must sound! I would cringe from such condescension, except that this was simply a matter of taste. Their taste was different to the one I knew; mine was alien to their concept of cleanliness.

The same applied to food. Apart from the Chinese restaurants within a few minutes' walk from Narrow Street – the Old Friends, the New Friends and the Friendly House – which served the best Chinese food I have tasted in my life, there were few good restaurants.

Doubtlessly transformed since then, the Indian restaurant in West India Dock Road was notable only for its cockroaches which decorated the walls in such profusion that I did not return after one of the most revolting meals I have known.

Needing food one evening, with a sudden, insatiable appetite for chicken, I found one at last, in a Jewish caff in Bethnal Green, which had been drained of blood according to the Hebrew ritual and was tasteless in consequence, to my palate at least.

Blooms in Whitechapel High Street was another matter, probably the only East End restaurant of repute and much beloved by its regulars for its traditional Jewish food. It was described memorably as 'the one restaurant in London where rich and poor all eat together, remembering their past or speculating on each other's future'. *The Good Food Guide* added the comment that 'They eat, and talk, rapidly and untidily,' admitting that the *Guide* had been rebuked for its sentimentality over Blooms by those who complained of the 'boorishness', 'the awful roast lamb' and the tepid food. I was promised the sort of meal cooked by a Jewish mother, and though I could not vouch for that I chose the legendary salt beef and decided yet again that this is not one of my favourite foods.

I far preferred the sea food from Tubby Isaacs' stall near by at Aldgate. This was a tradition which went back a hundred years to the streetsellers of hot pea soup and hot eels described by Henry Mayhew a hundred years ago 'as spicy as any in London, as if there was gin in it', according to 'a juvenile customer'. Mayhew recorded that on Saturdays, 100 pounds of eels were sold by the hot-eel man and his son, elegantly dressed in Jenny Lind hats bound with blue velvet, while his daughter washed the cups. The poorest, with a halfpenny to spend, but also those with means preferred the stalls to the restaurants. The eels were bought in Billingsgate early in the morning, and the watermen rowed them to the Dutch vessels moored off-shore. Half a dozen slices of hot eel, and three-quarters of a cupful of liquor, cost a halfpenny, and the whelks were sold according to size from a halfpenny each, and put out in saucers. Whelks were sealed in jars, ready to be 'shelled' into saucers. 'Whelks is all the same, good, bad, or middling,' said a customer, 'when a man's drinking, if they're well seasoned with pepper and vinegar.'

The ritual had scarcely changed, and my friends used to pause at Aldgate on their way from the West End to Limehouse.

The Eel-and-Pie Shops

I understood the preference for the gas-lit open stall to the grander version of the eel-and-pie shop, though this was another tradition spoken of with reverence, especially by those who rarely ate in them but admired the decor of such emporiums as Bob Cooke's, who advertised 'Hot Stewed Eels and Mashed Potato', with 'Live Eels Always' written underneath. The tiled interiors were undeniably ornate, but they reminded me of Turkish baths or public conveniences, and I have an aversion to food dolloped from metal containers which remind me of school, the army or an office canteen. As I disliked the idea of stewed eel in the first place, even with a parsley sauce, these were not the places for me.

Indeed, apart from those splendid Chinese restaurants, East End food was a disappointment – even at parties, where drink would be served lavishly, food was confined to pyramids of tasteless sandwiches.

The Markets of the East

Yet the markets, including those which sold the food initially, proved irresistible. Billingsgate was the brightest. And though the point might be absurd, I like the idea that a tang of the sea created a breezier atmosphere than the heavier roast beef of Old England sold at Smithfield. Billingsgate swanked that it was the finest fish market in the world.

In the early days it was frequented by fisherwomen who drank rum and fought like men. Hogarth's splendid portrait of *The Shrimp Girl*, referred to as *The Market Wench* by Mrs Hogarth, in the National Gallery, with the platter of red-brown shrimps perched upon her head, is the embodiment of a cockney girl's gaiety.

Even now Billinsgate retained the joyful noisy atmosphere described by Mayhew

Now the fishwives had gone but the humour remained, with the flat head-rests of the porters or 'Bummarees' supporting a pyramid of boxes, as they indulged in a roisterous repartee of a brand you would never find in the National Westminster Bank.

I went to Billingsgate to film Billy Walker, for this was a training-ground for young boxers who stretched their muscles as they hoisted the boxes of fish, with much of the work in the open air near the river. Equally, it could be the graveyard for the could-have-beens of the treacherous world of boxing, and the 'punchies' who may even have been champions once but were now worn out and lingered for the odd jobs which earned them the price of a pint or two. At the bottom of the pile, the methylated-spirit drinkers walked from Itchy Park and Whitechapel in the early hours and, for a few pennies, pushed the barrows up an incline known poignantly as 'the hill of despair'.

The finest account of East End street life can be found in Henry Mayhew's *London Labour and the London Poor*, published in 1851 and many times revised. The blurb on my edition states: 'It is not a pretty picture, far too often it is coloured by squalor and misery, yet in spite of every adversity the cockney's humour inevitably shines through the clouds of human suffering.' This expressed my own feelings a hundred years later though I flinched from the well-intended comment in the *Oxford Mail* in 1960 that 'Henry Mayhew, a nineteenth-century journalist and a sort of forerunner of the Dan Farsons of television, carried out social investigations among men and women who earned their living in the streets of London.' Complimentary to us; deeply condescending to Mayhew whose work was on a prodigious, detailed scale, though he never lost his zest for the ways of life he witnessed.

Mayhew advised his readers to visit Billingsgate at its busiest 'costermonger' time at seven o'clock in the morning, 'coster' referring to the street-vendors who sold their wares from barrows. The market opened at four, thronged to start with by the fishmongers and bummarees who had the best of the pick. Then as many as 4,000 costermongers descended:

> As soon as you reach the Monument you see a line of them, with one or two tall fishmonger's carts breaking the uniformity, and the din of the cries and commotion of the distant market begins to break on the ear like the buzzing of a hornet's nest. The whole neighbourhood is covered with the hand-barrows, some laden with baskets, others with sacks. Yet as you walk along, a fresh line of costers' barrows are creeping in or being backed into almost impossible openings; until at every turn nothing but donkeys and rails are to be seen. The morning air is filled with a kind of seaweedy odour, reminding one of the sea-shore; and on entering the market, the smell of fish, of whelks, red herrings, sprats, and a hundred others, is almost overpowering.

Red herrings! I thought they were the work of fiction. Mayhew had the rare genius to combine his observation with such a vivid style that one can picture the scene he evoked:

> the tangled rigging of the oyster boats and the red worsted caps of the sailors. Over the hum of voices is heard the shouts of the salesmen, who, with their white aprons peering above the heads of the mob, stand on their tables, roaring out their prices. All are bawling together – salesmen and hucksters of provisions, capes, hardware and newspapers – till the place is a perfect Babel of competition. 'Ha-a-ansome cod! Best in the market! All alive! Alive! Alive O!'

At that time oysters were so plentiful that they were the diet of East Enders, with costers naming the line of moored oyster boats as Oyster Street. Yarmouth bloaters were abundant and lobsters were plentiful, described by Mayhew as 'lying on the white bellies of the turbots . . . intensely scarlet from the contrast', another phrase as fresh as the fish he wrote about.

On my arrival the scene had scarcely changed, though the prices were higher and the oysters were now the diet of the rich.

This vitality could be found in all the markets of the East End; and, judging by the crowds of people who wandered through them with wide-eyed curiosity, I was not alone in finding them irresistible.

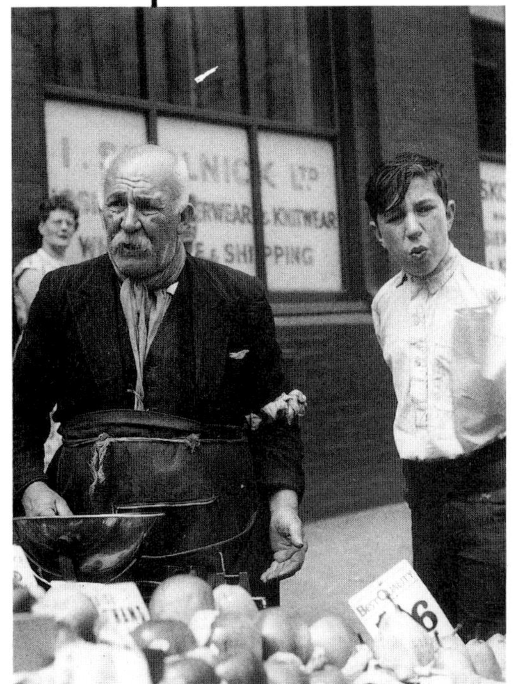

PEANUT QUEEN OF ALDGATE
AGENT FOR
FRESH ROASTED PEANUTS

WATNEYS
PETTICOAT LANE M

It is hard to tell why a market, with the refuse at one's feet, is more romantic than a shopping precinct, but it is – immeasurably. I have wandered contentedly with my camera through the souks of Fez and Marrakesh, and some of my best and earliest photographs were taken at the flea-market in Paris where the open-fronted shops were arranged like stage-sets with statuary and life-size Hussars in uniform, and forlorn men sitting by open suitcases which displayed a couple of bananas on the lid, at the other end of the scale.

The markets of the East End were equally spectacular, especially on a Saturday night in Mayhew's time, when he compared the character to that of a fairground.

> There are hundreds of stalls, and every stall has one or two lights; either it is illuminated by the intense white light of the new self-generating gas-lamp, or else it is brightened up by the red smoky flame of the old-fashioned grease lamp. One man shows off his yellow haddock with a candle stuck in a bundle of firewood; his neighbour makes a candlestick of a huge turnip, and the tallow gutters over its sides; whilst the boy shouting 'Eight a penny, stunning pears!' has rolled his dip in a thick coat of brown paper, that flares away with the candle.
>
> The pavement and the road are crowded with purchasers and street-sellers. The housewife in her thick shawl, with the market-basket on her arm, walks slowly on, stopping now to look at the stall of caps, now to cheapen a bunch of greens. Little boys holding three or four onions in their hand, creep between the people, wriggling their way through every interstice, and asking for custom in whining tones as if for charity. Then the tumult of the thousand different cries of the eager dealers, all shouting at the top of their voices, at one and the same time, is almost bewildering.

Inevitably when I was there they were less raucous, but I found the atmosphere much the same, especially in Petticoat Lane with its vociferous bargaining. There was also a sense of desperation. It was never a pretty market and behind the lively humour I detected a calculated aggression, even from the blind beggars who advanced forbiddingly with their musical instruments as if they were weapons. It occurred to me that if I slipped on the decaying rubbish, I could be crushed underfoot. Yet this was part of the attraction: markets should not be pretty but places of mutual gain and greed as each side hopes to cheat the other.

I was surprised by the similar paucity of the articles on sale, scarcely superior to the matchboxes, mouse traps and metal spoons in Mayhew's day, with secondhand clothes replaced by items straight from the factory, even if they had fallen off the back of the proverbial lorry.

Mayhew made the shrewd observation that the distinctive character of the street trade was reflected equally by 'what is *not* sold and not encouraged. I saw no old books.' Nor did I. Sadly, the East End did not boast a single bookshop.

Another East End observer, Walter Besant, described the market at the turn of the century, halfway between Mayhew's experience and my own, stressing that Sunday morning in Wentworth Street, Middlesex Street and the old Petticoat Lane was the time to see the poorer Jews of London gathered together:

> Sunday is their market day; all the shops are open; the streets are occupied by a triple line of stalls, on which are exposed for sale all kinds of things, but chiefly garments – coats and trousers. There is a mighty hubbub of those who chaffer and those who offer and those who endeavour to attract attention.
>
> They know the tricks, they have learned the art. One wonders how many such fervid speeches this young man has to make before he effects a single sale. We need not pity him, although at the close of the market his voice is hoarse with bawling and the result is meagre; he enjoys the thing; it is his one day of glory, and he has many admirers . . .
>
> Not all the holders of stalls are so eloquent. Here, before a miserable tray resting on crazy trestles, stand a ragged old couple. They look very, very poor; they cast wistful eyes upon the heedless crowd; their wares are nothing but common slippers of bright red and blue cloth. Will you buy a pair because the makers are so old? Alas! they cannot understand your offer; their only language is Yiddish, that remarkable composite tongue which in one place is a mixture of Russian and Hebrew, in another of German and Hebrew, in another of Lettish and Hebrew. [Lett denotes people from the Baltic.]
>
> They stare, they eagerly offer their wares; a kindly compatriot from the crowd interprets. There is a little bargaining and the slippers are in your pocket. It is a piece of good luck for the old pair . . . they will dine today. True to their national instincts which are Oriental, they have made you pay three times as much for the slippers as they would charge one of their own people. Going on slowly with the crowd one admires the variety of the wares laid out on trestles. Who wants these rusty iron things – keys, locks, broken tools, things unintelligible?
>
> Somebody, for there is noisy chaffering.

On Saturdays the Jews still observed their laws so religiously that I was told they paid Christian boys to put logs on their fires rather than tend to them personally. But on Sunday mornings such markets as the one in Hessel Street were active. Steven Berkoff has written that Hessel Street 'could have been torn out of a European ghetto – a dense soup of languages with Yiddish being the unifying one. It was straight out of Isaac Singer. Old bent backs sold bagels in the street out of giant sacks.'

When I went there for last-minute additions to Sunday lunch, I was offered bagels from large wicker baskets, and continued back to the House of Frumkin around the corner in Commercial Road, where I ordered wine and was offered a small glass of cherry brandy and a slice of excellent fruit cake.

On Saturday mornings I went to the market at Bermondsey, a modest version of the Paris flea-market and still rich enough in bric-à-brac to find Victorian antiques – flower-pieces made from small white shells, even a stuffed canary, protected by tall glass domes. And personal mementoes which had meant so much to someone once and were now discarded for a few shillings, like the record of a 'Cruise in China and Japan', with the sailor's photograph flanked by embroidered flags and the inscription above the crown, 'England Expects that Every Man This Day Will Do His Duty'.

It was still possible to find bargains in Bermondsey, although it never achieved the fame of the Paris flea market

On Sundays, East Enders revealed their sentimentality as they flocked to the flower market in Columbia Road, the men in greater numbers than the women, returning home with a clutched plant pot as a guilt offering before the lunchtime session in the pub from which the wives were excluded.

These markets confirmed the successful absorption of the Jews, with the second generation regarding themselves as English. Writing of Wentworth Street as far back as 1893, an architect called Robert Williams doubted if there was any part of the world so fascinating when 'the market in the street is in full swing':

> A street like this, cut out as it were, from the thick of Jerusalem, is what makes one love old England. The roots of freedom are here, say what we will about the alien. He is welcome, and ever may it be so.

Would that East End tolerance were still so strong.

Cockney Sparrows

Cockney rhyming slang was another form of release, invented in prison as a code to confuse the warders. Some of the origins are intricate to the point of peculiarity; even 'cockney' is convoluted, apparently derived from a 'cock's egg – small and ill-shaped'. 'Harris' was derived from Aristotle: hence bottle and glass = arse. 'What are they doing thinking about that in prison?' asked Michael Caine with startling naivety; surely the knowledge of Aristotle was the more extraordinary.

'Iron' struck me as equally archaic: iron hoof = poof. *Iron hoof!* It conjures up a clattering image of horses and highwaymen – poofy highwaymen, perhaps?

Another bizarre euphemism is 'berk', used by comedians on television without the faintest idea of its meaning. Even Mr Berkeley of Berkeley Castle was astonished when I explained that East Enders, like Americans, pronounce Berkeley as Burkley. When you realise that 'berk' is derived from the Berkeley Hunt, you will understand why Mr Berkeley was dismayed.

Some euphemisms are worse than the words they are disguising, with the awkward gentility of 'What about a quick Donald?', 'a gypsy's kiss' or 'Jimmy Riddle', and an Eartha Kitt, to describe some bodily functions which you can work out for yourself.

Masturbation is celebrated with various versions of 'wank': a 'J. Arthur'; a 'Jodrell', with the addition of 'a load of Merchant Bankers' since the arrival of the Yuppies.

The cockney alphabet starts with A for horses; B for mutton; C for Miles; and D for Nition, with a few wittier exceptions, such as I for Novello; L for leather; and R for Askey, now replaced by Daley.

Mayhew confirms that cockney slang was equally obscure a century earlier: 'The slang language of the costermongers is not very remarkable for originality of construction; it possesses no humour . . .' He proves this with such examples as 'Flatch' for halfpenny, and 'Yenep-flatch' for three-half-pence; though 'Flatch kanurd' meaning half-drunk, has a nice ring to it, as does 'tumble to your barrikin' for 'understand you'.

Getting Away

Even those who were proud to live in the East End were glad to get away. The goals were the seaside and the open country, exemplified by Marie Lloyd with such songs as 'Saturday to Monday', to which she added a wealth of suggestion:

Oh, will you come with me
To Brighton on the sea
And will you go upon my yacht on Sunday?
If you'll only say the word,
I'll take you like a bird,
And bring you safely back to town on Monday.

The country was hardly immortalised with the lyrics:

We went gathering carslips
Moo-cow came to me
Wagged 'is apparatus
And I said unto he
Rumptiddly – umptiddley ... etc ...

It was Mark Sheridan who came closest to that with 'I do like to be beside the seaside'.

Always one to have her cake and eat it, Marie combined her fondness for the country and for water too, by buying two houseboats which she moored at Staines: for the day, *The Sunbeam* and for the night *The Moonbeam*, which slept seven and sank one night in three feet of water. 'Then believe me, we heard all about it from Marie!' said Johnny Wood, her brother. 'The beauties of the river, the joys of having houseboats. But she always loved it, and I think those days were the happiest of her life.'

For most cockneys the outlets were simpler: Southend or hopping.

Southend represented the ocean with the longest pier in the world, over a mile with a single-track railway and views over the mud-flats or 'sandy approaches'. The pier had been extended in 1909 to accommodate the steam pleasure boats which came from Greenwich.

In 1919, *The Southend and Westcliff Graphic* took a swipe at the cockney, declaring that 'It would be the height of folly to carry on the evil tradition of the past century, during which period Southend became the synonym for cockneydom and was the paradise of the day tripper. That era is dead, and we hope it will never be resurrected.'

What pretension! The tradition was far from dead, for day-trippers flocked to Southend when I was there, especially at the weekend.

The pier was once so elegant that the *Graphic* in its snobbery hoped it would deter 'the malodorous Whitechapel element'. A massive pavilion included restaurants, a ballroom and a theatre, while the music halls, public houses and side-shows provided entertainment on shore for the visitor that was more robust. The *Graphic* notwithstanding, a jolly time was had by all – especially the malodorous lot from Whitechapel.

Yet East Enders have always been treated with suspicion. Poverty, like disease, was disagreeable and warned of failure. A popular image was that of a blowsy woman with a black eye, sitting on a doorstep in a white apron shelling peas, with her husband's explanation - 'If you didn't give 'em a black eye on Saturday night, they'd think you didn't love them any more.'

Animals!

When Charles Kingsley used the word 'cockney' as early as 1864 he did so in a derogatory context: 'How goes the Northam Burrows Scheme for spoiling the beautiful place with hotels and villas?' he asked of a friend, deploring the creation of *Westward Ho!* which was named after his novel. 'You will frighten away all the seapies and defile the Pebble Ridge with chicken bones and sandwich scraps. The universe is growing cockney, and men like me must look for a new place to live in.'

This was an unfair dig at the cockney's craving for the open air and the seaside in particular, but it is undeniable that cockneys were regarded with alarm.

Hopping conjures up an image of greater innocence, a respite for the family and the women and the girls in particular, with the chance to get away from the Smoke.

East Enders looked forward to the cockney holiday in September: two or three weeks' hopping in Kent, where they stripped the vines. As many as 80,000 travelled to Kent when hopping had its heyday, though the acreage of hops gradually decreased from 71,327 in 1835 to under 50,000 in 1903. The change was inevitable but the tradition continued into the 1920s, as Louis Heren reveals in his autobiography. Most of the hoppers came on special trains which ran from London Bridge, or by lorry; there would have been scenes worthy of Hogarth as the hoppers assembled with bundles of bedding and sacks of possessions, boxes with pails and frying pans, for they could not afford proper luggage, the men in their work clothes, with the women armoured in black pinafores, shawls and caps.

They slept in sheds and hopped by day. At night the men drank in the pubs which allowed them in, though many had signs in the windows stating that hoppers and gypsies would not be allowed, for the prejudice against the cockney existed even here. Only breakfast was cooked; lunch was bottled tea and bread and cheese. It was dismally uncomfortable when it rained and the reward was hardly lavish however welcome: a few shillings according to weight.

Yet this is an idealistic image; there was another view. Jack London described the cockney visitors: 'They are out of place. As they drag their squat misshapen bodies along the highways and byways, they resemble some vile spawn from underground.' London reflected the common antipathy rather than his own, though he had experienced hop-picking for himself. Walter Besant, moderate as always, admitted that Maidstone Gaol had been filled with hoppers charged with being drunk and disorderly in the autumn of 1898, and referred to the lack of cleanliness in the camps. Local headlines protested, 'Tramps plentiful, hops few'.

But Besant added the poignant footnote that 'the roadway outside the principal station for their return was observed to be strewn with the old boots discarded by the hoppers when they bought new ones on their way home.' New boots! That was a positive step forward, and like the holiday-makers today who return from the Costa Brava to impress the neighbours with their tan, the hoppers struggled back to the East End weary but content with the superiority of red cheeks and sunburnt noses. Yet glad to be home: to quote the words of Marie's 'Coster Girl in Paris', 'Born and bred down 'Ackney Road, ah! an' proud to own it too.'

Towards the end of my biography of Henry Williamson, the naturalist and author of *Tarka the Otter*, I quoted his dismay when he described a visit to the countryside one Sunday in May 1920, joining an invasion of East Enders:

> The paths were beaten into mire by the passing and repassing of a thousand feet, acres of bluebells had been uprooted and taken away, many trampled and crushed, or gathered and carelessly cast on the paths. The apple blossom was stripped from the trees ... the blooms were gone, a whole spring-life of them, carried away by the people who had come from Walworth, Shoreditch, and Woolwich.

Henry walked unhappily to the tram terminus for the journey back, with the East Enders clutching their symbols of spring:

> I looked at the transfigured faces of the children – old or young they were all children – who breathed in the smoke and worked in the shadow, and saw that the beauty of the wild flowers had passed into their eyes; although the woods were ravaged, the spoiling and pillaging had not been in vain.

And Henry was filled with ecstasy. He was a fine enough naturalist to know that people came first, but the East Enders had a greater innocence then.

12

GETTING ON, GETTING OUT – AND THE EAST END ARTISTS

FOR A LUCKY few, talent offered the chance of escape. Some cockneys found overnight success: like Charles Chaplin, born north of the river. He worked on the same bill as Marie Lloyd when he was a boy and remembered 'this anxious, plump little lady pacing nervously up and down behind the scenes, irritable and apprehensive until the moment for her to go on. Then she was immediately gay and relaxed.' By the time I arrived, it was Pop which offered fame and fortune as the member of a group, or hairdressing.

If you got on, you got out. Those who had 'made it' in the East End were glad to move to somewhere posh, especially the third-generation Jew who preferred the duller prosperity of the suburbs. Marie Lloyd scarpered to Golders Green; and though H. M. Tomlinson, author of such romantic novels as *The Sea and the Jungle*, wrote, 'Cut the kind of life you find in Poplar, and I must bleed', he left it and his job as a shipping clerk in the docks as soon as his writing enabled him to do so.

Tomlinson was one of the few writers produced by the East End, but the area produced a number of formidable artists – David Bomberg and Isaac Rosenberg in the past; Leon Kossoff; Bert Irvin; Paul Caro; Shafique Uddin, a young Bangladesh painter who depicts the East End scene; and Vincent Milne with his views of Dockland today.

The Whitechapel Art Gallery has encouraged such artists since it was founded at the end of the last century by the discerning educationalist the Rev. Samuel Augustus Barnett, usually known as Canon Barnett. When he informed the Bishop of London that he wished to go East to Whitechapel, the Bishop viewed this unusual shift with alarm, urging him not to be hasty: 'It is the worst parish in my diocese.' The Barnetts were forewarned yet not deterred. Describing their arrival at their proposed home, Mrs Barnett related:

> it was market day and the main street was filled with hay carts, entangled among which were scores of frightened cattle being driven to the slaughter house. The people were dirty and bedraggled, the children neglected, the beer shops full, the schools shut up. I can recall the realisation of the immensity of our task and the fear of failure to reach or to help these crowds of people, with vice, woe and lawlessness written across their faces.

This was exactly what Canon Barnett had been hoping for. 'We came to Whitechapel attracted by its poverty and ambitious to fight it in its strongest fortress.'

In her perceptive tribute to Barnett in *This is Whitechapel*, Helen Sachs referred to such Jeremiahs as Professor Huxley who compared the East Enders of the last century with 'brutish island dwellers before the missionaries', while having no illusions concerning Barnett's kinder yet blinkered approach, judging it in the context of his time:

> Intellectual modesty and doubt were not qualities which most Victorians possessed – and Samuel Barnett was no exception. It was one of their many social and political misconceptions that poverty would be erased by improving the minds of the poor rather than their material conditions. Canon Barnett's main concern was with spiritual turpitude and deprivation, yet he was for an idealist, an unusually practical man.

In 1877 Barnett confirmed his intention

> to decrease not suffering but sin. Too often has East London been described as if its inhabitants were pressed down by poverty and every spiritual effort which has been made for its reformation has been supported by means which aim only at reducing suffering.
>
> In my eyes the pain which belongs to the winter cold is not so terrible as the drunkenness with which the summer heat fills our streets. The want of clothes does not call so loudly for remedy as does the want of interest and culture. It is sin therefore in its widest sense that we are here to fight. Sin in the sense of missing the Best.

One can imagine the disgust of the Whitechapel poor when he offered them culture rather than clothing, and art instead of food. Yet Barnett's belief that 'love [which] strengthens character' may have been naive but achieved a lasting good. He became the first Warden of Toynbee Hall (a university settlement for social reform), and after he opened the neglected schoolrooms behind the vicarage he held the first art exhibitions which led to the construction of the Whitechapel Art Gallery in 1901.

When he died in 1913, an obituary said he had changed the face of East

London, and he was undeniably one of its great reformers. Since he came from the West, a place was reserved for him in Westminster Abbey where he ended his life as a Canon, but he had chosen to return to the East End and be buried in the grounds of St Jude's Church in Whitechapel, faithful to the end to the wilder parish of his adoption.

Over the years the Whitechapel Art Gallery has expanded: now it includes workshops and the East End Open Studios where local artists show their work. There is even a café and a first-rate bookshop run by Zwemmer's. The Gallery has also indulged in the necessary panache. In the 1950s and 60s, Bryan Robertson exhibited work by Pollok and Raushenberg; Mark Glazebrook organised the first large show by David Hockney in 1970; and Jenny Stein invited Leon Kossoff to exhibit in 1972, closer to home. Nicholas Serota brought Kiefer, Baselitz, Hodgkin and Schnabel to the Whitechapel between 1976 and 1988, which introduced controversy, at the least, in the tradition of a Gallery which dared to exhibit Picasso's *Guernica* in 1939. Nicholas Serota moved to the Tate Gallery in 1988, which he has since transformed, succeeded at Whitechapel by Catherine Lampert who has been a resident of the East End for the last eighteen years.

On the steps of Spitalfields church, the artists Gilbert and George, who have made their home in Fournier Street, originally lived in by Huguenots

Today there are numerous studios in the area, including the Lamont Gallery which specialises in exhibitions by artists who record the East End.

I 'discovered' a painter myself: Dick Whyte, who worked as a rigger in the West India Docks and was born and bred in Poplar. He started painting in 1959 by accident, when his father who made model boats as a hobby had some paint to spare and Dick experimented with a picture. I saw it and a couple of others in the Gun on the Isle of Dogs and asked if I could meet him.

A broad man with a turned-up nose and curly hair falling over his forehead, he had the look of a calf taken by surprise. He was immensely likable and friendly and the last thing he wanted to talk about was painting, steering the conversation towards his new flat, local pubs, or his experience with the Army in Italy, though his eyes absorbed the scene around him as he was talking.

I expressed my admiration for the freshness of his work and asked for more, even commissioning a lengthy view of Greenwich for the pub I had taken over up the road (described at length in Chapter 14).

Dick Whyte was far from keen, protesting that he was not really a painter and had no experience. It was true that he painted only what he knew – tugs, barges, ships and cranes. A later view from my balcony at Narrow Street revealed a passing cargo boat from Rotterdam, a modern version of the *Marie Celeste* with not a soul in sight, apparently self-propelled. Yet, when he dared to paint the interior of the Waterman's Arms at a later date, he was forced to fill it with customers and it was bought immediately.

Dick Whyte, the East End painter, in Charley Brown's pub

Dick Whyte worked happily in the evening at home, on hardboard treated with Polyseal and white emulsion paint, surrounded by his children and his wife Rose.

'It's relaxing,' he explained, 'like fishing.' Though he enjoyed the attention it made him bemused as well, and so nervous that when he took part in a television interview for *Tonight* I had to escort him to the lavatory beforehand where he was desperately sick.

Because he was true to himself alone, I promoted Dick Whyte as a 'primitive' which attracted immediate attention; and I accompanied Godfrey Winn when he decided to write him up and drove from the West End in his Daimler to interview him in his 'riverside home': 'The two little girls were squatting on the floor, playing with crayons, their eldest sister was watching television, their pretty mother, with the rather delicate features, was sewing in the chair by the fire; their father was still in his working clothes, with a wide leather belt holding up his blue dungarees. He couldn't have looked less like the Bohemian image of an artist.'

When Whyte produced some of his canvases with the greatest reluctance, Winn asked how he achieved such 'perspective' and 'patina'. Dick scratched his mop of hair uncomfortably: 'I dunno. I just dig in and start with the sky, and then somehow everything seems to come right.'

'We went downstairs again,' wrote Winn, 'and I told myself it looks like the interior of any one of twenty houses in the row. But there is this difference, this unexpected, inexplicable talent. How, why does it happen?'

Throughout the visit Godfrey Winn had behaved like royalty with an attentive condescension as if he were inspecting a show of local crafts, as indeed he was, and though this appalled me it thrilled the Whytes. 'What a very nice gentleman,' Mrs Whyte told me afterwards, and she was right. To do him justice, Winn was more appreciative, wiser and kinder than his reputation suggested, and he knew this was an occasion for the family and that he should rise to it accordingly.

I had been relieved when Dick Whyte told Winn that his pictures were starting to sell, but he would never give up his job in the docks. I suspect he was too guileless to become a great artist, yet too proficient to be acclaimed as an artistic oddity like Alfred Wallis, the Cornish 'naif'. His painting was a happy pastime for himself and gave pleasure to those who saw them – I still have two in my possession; yet I believe I might feel guiltier if I had promoted him to greater success for he was content as he was, and that was priceless.

Though it is presumptuous to name one artist as 'the best' in preference to another, I believe it would be fair to claim that apart from David Bomberg, Mark Gertler was the leading artist created by the East End.

Gertler is a classic example of someone who was forged by his surroundings, moved out, and was ultimately destroyed.

Self-portrait by Mark Gertler

Mark Gertler was born in the East End in 1891 after his 24-year-old mother emigrated from Galicia in Eastern Europe, but she was so poor that she was forced to return to her homeland, assisted by the London Jewish Board. The family struggled back six years later and this time they stayed, looking so forlorn as they emerged from Liverpool Street station that strangers threw them coins.

Recalling his first night in a Shoreditch tenement, Gertler experienced 'the first fit of depression that I consciously suffered'. The first of many.

Yet his was a case of talent and perseverance rising above adversity. Gertler bore the additional alienation of being Jewish in a family which observed the rules punctiliously, but it was these bonds which held them together. His mother, Golda, was a true matriarch who never learnt English; indeed when she carried him to his first Board School her accent was so impenetrable that the Inspector misheard his real name, which was Max, and wrote it down as Mark, which he became.

The family had arrived at a bad moment when the East End was besieged by a flood of migrants escaping from the Russian pogroms, with as many as 500 arriving at the Poor Jews Temporary Shelter in Leman Street on a single day.

Yet his down-trodden father kept the family together, sand-papering walking-sticks at 12*s.* 6*d.* a week. 'It was a poor wage,' wrote Gertler, 'yet we were all very cheerful, and very soon we were to have a home of our own. I can't imagine how it was managed on 12*s.* 6*d.* a week, but sure enough we got our home.' This consisted of a single room in Zion Square.

Gertler was an exceptionally bright, attractive boy, almost feminine as a young man though not effeminate, entertaining his fellow students with his mimicry of the turns he saw in the Music Halls. His father managed to send him to the Regent Street Polytechnic where he laid down the foundations of one of the fastest rises to fame for a young artist. When he appealed for help from the Jewish Educational Society at the age of seventeen, he was rejected by the artist Solomon J. Solomon but encouraged by William Rothenstein, who wrote to his father: 'It is never easy to prophesy regarding the future of an artist but I do sincerely believe that your son has gifts of a high order, and that if he will cultivate them with love and care, that you will one day have reason to be proud of him.' Golda had the letter framed and hung it in the kitchen.

Rothenstein persuaded the Slade School of Art to accept him, with a £35 yearly scholarship which alleviated the strain on his father. This was the start of Gertler's ascent, which is another story, told by Michael Holroyd in his life of Lytton Strachey, and by John Woodeson in his biography *Mark Gertler* (Sidgwick & Jackson, 1972) to which I am indebted.

Gertler became increasingly remote from his origins as he was taken up by the Bloomsbury set and 'nice friends among the upper class', such as Lady Ottoline Morrell – though she deserves credit for tracking down the talked-of protégé in the East End: 'I went off to Liverpool Street station and found my way from there to the mean, hot, stuffy, smelly little street where he lived. I felt very tall and large walking up the creaky little stairs.' When they met they became friends instantly and she launched him into the society which she ruled as a powerful hostess. Meanwhile, his friendships included such fellow artists as Christopher Nevinson, Stanley Spencer, Paul Nash and the strange girl with the short hair-cut, an artist called Dora Carrington, though she was known simply as Carrington. Obsessively in love, he wanted to marry her: 'You are to me the *one* thing outside painting worth living for.'

His most celebrated painting was the *Merry Go Round*, a biting indictment of the First World War with soldiers and sailors whirled around the carousel like robots. With the outbreak of the war he found himself hurled on to a merry-go-round in his personal life, which was equally fraught. Lytton Strachey made advances which he repelled, writing to Carrington: 'You can't think how uncomfortable it is for a *man* to feel that he is attracting another *man* that way ... to any decent man to attract another physically is simply revolting.' Perhaps Carrington could understand, for though she tried to respond to Gertler she was in love with Lytton Strachey and wanted to be a boy, dressing as one when they went on holiday as uncle and nephew – one of their happiest moments.

The permutations of their relationships, which have been recorded elsewhere, ended with Lytton Strachey's death, Carrington's suicide soon afterwards, and ultimately Gertler's suicide too, though he had married someone else.

What is relevant here are the doubts Gertler had in leaving the East End in the first place: 'I shall always be unhappy if I try to get away from this class to which I belong ... I must go on in the *East End*. There lies my work, sordid as it is.'

His fears were fulfilled when he was taken up by a smarter set and men like Edward Marsh, the secretary to Winston Churchill, who seems to have been in love with Gertler, though Cyril Connolly wrote that 'his prance was worse than his pounce'.

'Gertler is by birth an absolute little East End Jew,' wrote Marsh to Rupert Brooke. 'I am going to see him in Bishopsgate and be initiated into the ghetto. He is rather beautiful, and has a funny little shiny black fringe; his mind is deep and simple, and I think he's got the *feu sacré*!' He amplified that phrase with the declaration that Gertler was 'the greatest genius of the age', and, more helpfully, gave him a weekly allowance.

D. H. Lawrence was wiser in his assessment, writing of the *Merry Go Round*, which had prompted Strachey to exclaim 'Oh Lord Oh Lord have mercy upon us!':

> It would take a Jew to paint this picture ... At last your race is at an end – these pictures are its death cry. And it will be left for the Jews to utter the final and great death cry of this epoch. But I do think that in this combination of blaze and violent mechanical rotation ... and ghastly, utterly mindless human intensity of sensational extremity you have made a real and ultimate revelation. It is the best *modern* picture I have seen.

Lawrence added the prophetic warning: 'Take care or you will burn your flame so fast, it will suddenly go out.'

And it did. Gertler no longer belonged; he was *déraciné*.

13

Pubs in the Evening

MY EXPLORATION of the East End led me, not unwillingly, to the pubs. Apart from those outside the dock gates, these were cavernously empty at lunchtime. I had made the mistake a few years earlier of taking a bus to a popular pub in Hackney one Saturday lunchtime, a journey that took so long, with a maze of wrong directions, that I arrived there shortly before it closed for the afternoon. There was the additional disappointment of finding it empty, apart from an ill-tempered barman who replied 'Evenings' with a terseness I deserved when I asked if I had come to the right place. Surprisingly, I was accompanied on this abortive venture by Francis Bacon, who was equally engrossed by the unfamiliar landscape, and equally unworldly in assuming that Saturday lunchtimes in the East End would prove as crowded as they were 'up West'. Expressing some impatience with my stupidity, he managed to find a taxi to take us back to the Colony Room in Soho where we could drink in the afternoon. We did not return.

Now I discovered the numerous East End pubs which pulsated with live entertainment in welcome contrast to the taped Variety on television which had settled into a transatlantic rut.

Far from predictable, the entertainment ranged from modern jazz at Bermondsey (the south, and therefore the wrong side of the river), to stand-up comics and the female impersonators so beloved by the British.

I took Antony Armstrong-Jones and the actress Jacqui Chan to the Bridge House at Canning Town one Sunday lunchtime – Sundays were the festive exception – to join the crowd of dockers who cheered lustily a few minutes before closing time as the girl strippers removed every garment, and then staggered home to a late, traditional lunch. Armstrong-Jones wrote to me later that he had returned to the pub to find that the strip-tease had been replaced by elderly Indian fire-eaters: 'It was not the same.'

With pubs featuring their favourite turns, which attracted a following of regulars, it occurred to me that here was a form of Music Hall that had returned to its roots. There was the same challenge for the artist to establish himself immediately by sheer force of personality; also, a similar vulnerability, for though the pub performers had the armour of a microphone, they needed to rise above the clash and clatter of the crowd. Even more than with Music

Hall, the audience was part of the fun. There was no courtesy towards an indifferent performer who was drowned by noise, but if the customers took to an artist they listened attentively, though applause was sparse due to the difficulty of clapping with a beer mug in one hand. At least this was not chained to the seat as it had been in the rougher Halls where the orchestra was protected from a hail of trotter bones by a mesh screen.

When an artist triumphed, the atmosphere was warm and the comments generous. Unlike the southern English who dared to be amused, the East Enders set out for the night determined to enjoy themselves, a quality they shared with the north. After all, what was the point of sinking to the occasion?

For me, the constant delight was the 'local talent': members of the audience who needed little prompting to get up on stage and perform, like the taxi-driver who impersonated the Al Jolson numbers whose sentimentality made them perennially popular. If the performers lacked refinement, they possessed a raw vitality which was more exciting than the images on television. By comparison, the West End nightclubs looked stale.

Ida Barr adding a touch of Music Hall, which started in the East End pubs

The pubs had the gusto of Music Hall and created their own stars: notorious for his cruelty to hecklers at the Deuragon, Ray Martine was the East End's answer to Lenny Bruce, acid, obscene, dislikable on stage and often difficult off it, and sometimes dangerous, thirty years before today's 'alternative comedians', though Martine subsequently appeared at the Establishment in Soho, as Bruce had done.

There was also Welsh George, a lanky, white-haired young man with an exotic, dark-haired beauty for his girlfriend. He would lean on his stick as he poured out his heart for his 'Yiddisher Mama' at the Rising Sun at Bethnal Green where he was the compère, introducing such acts as Tex, the East End cowboy – a hunchback who wore a massive stetson, accompanied on stage by a white horse, singing ballads about his best friend, usually a dog or the horse itself.

If the Rising Sun was an East End Palladium, the Ironbridge sustained the 'Blues'. At the near end of the iron bridge that led to the Bridge House and Canning Town, with a desolate yet fascinating landscape stretching behind it with the winding River Lea and factory chimneys, the Ironbridge was managed by Slim and Queenie Watts. 'Slim' was a tall, rugged, laconic man, a sort of East End Robert Mitchum, an inveterate gambler and heavy drinker who kept remarkably fit by restricting his diet for several days to liquids. Queenie sang the Blues so powerfully that I made the Ironbridge a regular destination on Sunday lunchtimes, for the last half-hour at least. She had the ability to galvanise the most jaded atmosphere, with the resilience of the East Ender determined to have a good time against the odds.

She was christened 'Mary', a memory which appalled her: 'Sadie, yes! But not Mary. Why, if people had called me that, I might have been a teacher. I must tell you the absolute truth – my father was a gypsy and I had the darkest eyes, and in his dear old-fashioned way he said, "One day she'll be the Queen of the gypsies." '

Her mother was a singer who made her dance and sing on the tops of tables with her sister while her mother yelled instructions – 'Open your mouth' – 'Move your body', and when she mispronounced words – 'bu-er' instead of 'butter' – wham! a cane descended on their fingers.

This accounted for her precise way of talking.

'Have you always got your own way?' I asked.

'Since I've been married.'

She met Jim, nicknamed 'Slim', at a dance hall: 'He was stone drunk, dear, not dancing at all, with a lovely black eye. I always fall for a drunk. I was fourteen and he was fifteen, a boy on a training ship. They put him up against a mast and flogged him while someone held his hands.'

'But I thought that went out years ago!'

'Oh, it wasn't the authorities who flogged him, it was his own father, dear.'

'But why?'

'Someone hit him and he didn't hit back. Of course, dear, he always hit back after that.'

Their courtship was tempestuous. Jim returned from sea having spent most of his wages on a bracelet for her. Hurrying along the docks to find her, he saw Queenie on the other side of the road with another man and threw the bracelet into the canal.

'We made it up the next night. Eight of his friends had just paid off their ships and were they celebrating! I was the only girl but they brought me along as I played the piano. It was a right old session. There was a bench outside the pub and Jim ended up by rolling under it. It was ever so embarrassing as there was a courting couple on top. I had to go up and say, "Excuse me, but my fellow's under your seat."'

When they got married, Slim went into the scrap business and they made enough to become tenants of their own pub: 'where all the wonderful things can happen – crowds, music, laughs.' Queenie built her own group and her reputation grew by word of mouth: 'Today, if you don't put on a good show, you don't get the custom.'

A particular pleasure in life is the chance to reciprocate. I have been able to return some of the hospitality I receive in Turkey by expressing my appreciation in print. After moving to Limehouse, I was able to help people like Queenie Watts by giving them the moment of fame they hoped for, however short-lived.

Queenie Watts

When I was interviewed by Michael Ingrams in his series *To Stay Alive*, I suggested the Ironbridge as a setting, with Queenie belting out the blues. I witnessed an example of the West End misconception when Ingrams, a highly civilised man, hurried up as I was talking to a docker and his wife, telling them, 'You can't be in this shot, you look too glamorous. People will think this is the West End.' I tried to explain that East Enders were infinitely smarter than West Enders, who dressed down for the occasion, but a group of men in cloth caps were found and substituted instead.

I suggested a play to a leading television producer based on Joan Littlewood's concept of the East End called *Lovely Villains*, in which she filmed gangsters in a pub, with cloth caps and mufflers, while the real villains watched with astonishment, dressed impeccably. Kenneth Trodd, the producer, did not find this amusing, but the days of the cloth caps had gone and it was the visiting West Ender who stood out as badly dressed. Because I hate wearing a tie unless I have to, I was often asked 'Why do you look so scruffy, Dan?' To which someone else once replied, with one of the nicest compliments I have received, 'Leave orf, he's one of our own, even if he don't look like it.' The East Enders expected one to wear one's *best*, and were baffled by the sweaters, jeans and head-scarves worn by tourists who stared at each other in the Prospect of Whitby wondering who was 'local'.

Queenie and Slim became close friends. Once she confided in me: 'I'd like to have been a man, dear, absolutely, I'd never have married and I'd have spent a life at sea. The only time I like being a woman is when I get lovely presents.' She sweetened her voice as Slim joined us: 'If you bought me a mink coat this weekend, I'd be content to be a woman for the rest of my life.' His answer is unprintable.

I introduced Queenie to Joan Littlewood, who included her in *Sparrers* with a 'mock-up' of the Ironbridge in the studio where her performance was lost in the surrounding uproar of a bar-room brawl as the film reached its climax.

Fortunately, however, I was able to give her a greater opportunity when I took over a pub of my own.

14

Going to the Dogs

MY DECISION TO run a pub of my own happened by chance.

I had conceived the idea for a television programme on the boom in pub entertainment, with the ironic justice of showing the 'live' performers that television had replaced.

The idea met with a lukewarm reception in Television House – 'Why show a lot of amateurs?', was the gloomy comment from the cameraman. 'But if one of them is a welder, I suppose I could cut away to a shot of him welding while he sings.' I flinched.

'We don't want to make a programme,' added the Head of Entertainment, 'which is so boring that people turn off their sets.'

'No,' I agreed, 'that was not exactly my intention.'

When Rollo Gamble, the director I worked with, came to see the pubs for himself, he understood. 'But they're *marvellous*!' he enthused afterwards.

'That's what I've been trying to tell everyone.'

Due to his encouragement, we were allowed ahead. While I planned the programme which we were going to call *Time Gentlemen Please!*, I visited other pubs and continued my exploration of the river; and I found a little-used slipway at the far end of the Isle of Dogs, near the Park of the Isles opposite Greenwich. Playing contentedly in the mud were a group of grubby children, whose father was the landlord of a pub called the Newcastle Arms at the top. I returned to the Newcastle when the tides permitted, and realised that something was mysteriously wrong. Not only was the Newcastle invariably empty: sometimes I had to knock to get in, and one evening when I brought some friends the landlord had to phone for a taxi to go to another pub to fetch our drinks. I asked him what was the matter.

The pub was 'on the floor', he told me with disgust, known to the islanders as 'the pub with no beer'. The brewers refused to give him further credit, and though he wanted to leave as soon as possible, no one had shown the slightest interest in taking it over. I should have been warned; but as I looked around me, liking the way it was built on two levels, I imagined it with the connecting wall knocked down so that you could look onto a stage as if it was a theatre.

Pondering the future in the bar of the Newcastle Arms

With my mind preoccupied by pub entertainment, it seemed logical to take over a pub of my own. Why not the Newcastle Arms?

The instant reply to that was the pub's position at the far end of the Isle of Dogs, on the way to nowhere, with only three regulars who supped a Guinness all night long. This was the reason why no one else wanted to have anything to do with it. Yet I had the arrogance to interpret this as a challenge, assuming that if it was 'on the floor' its fortunes could only improve. I failed to recognise that it makes more sense to take over a thriving concern than one that has failed. I day-dreamt in terms of Citizen Kane when he decided to take over a newspaper: I thought it *might be fun* to run a pub. I was as foolish as that.

If I had explored the Isle of Dogs from inland, instead of from the Thames, I might have been warned by the long, deserted streets and the general air of desolation, though I doubt if I would have taken heed. Surely the Isle of Dogs had potential? I knew little of the area, except that the horse-shoe shape beyond Limehouse was linked by docks and bridges at the base which gave the romantic aura of an island. Why was it called the Isle of *Dogs*? I learnt that there were several theories. The popular explanation is that Charles II kept his kennels there when he lived across the river at Greenwich Palace, in order to distance himself from the noise when his spaniels barked. One writer suggests it was named after the wildlife – Isle of Ducks; Pepys referred to the 'unlucky Isle of Dogs in a chill place, the morning cool, the wind fresh to our great discontent' which may have contributed to the disparaging phrase, 'going to the dogs'. Certainly it presented a forlorn aspect to sailors returning home from sea, little more than bleak marshland with prisoners hanging from gibbets along the shore, engulfed by water at every tide.

The version I prefer is that of the faithful dog which stayed by the body of his master who was killed in a fight with another waterman. When he was driven by hunger, the dog swam across to Greenwich where he was given scraps before returning to his vigil. One day he attacked a waterman with such ferocity that the man confessed to the murder and following the arrest the faithful dog became a hero; so the wasteland became known as the isle of the dog. Unlikely, but pleasing.

It was hard to credit that as late as 1800, the Chapel House was the only dwelling on the marshland. The place became populated with the construction of the West India Docks in 1802 (Import, Export and South) which unearthed such startling remains as the tusks of an elephant and a petrified forest buried yards below the watermark, possibly after an earthquake – described at the time as 'a mass of decayed twigs, leaves and branches, encompassing huge trunks, yet perfect in every fibre'. Yet even with the prosperity brought by the Docks, a contemporary made the comment that 'The cold and swampy character of this tract of land would appear repulsive to all thoughts of human habitation.'

In the middle of the last century the island enjoyed a brief prosperity from ship building, but even this enterprise was 'dogged' by bad luck. One of our most important ships was launched there, *The Great Eastern* – 'The celebrated and magnificent Iron Paddle and Screw Steam-ship built on the Thames from designs and under the personal supervision of the eminent Engineer Isambard Brunel, by the celebrated firm of Scott Russell & Co., in 1858'. The largest vessel ever constructed, it was partly submerged when it stuck in the Thames after its first launching from Millwall. The following year it was launched again, but as Jules Verne wrote in *A Floating City*, 'after twenty passages to England from America, one of which was marked by very serious disasters, the use of *The Great Eastern* was temporarily abandoned.'

Then it was used as a cable ship by a French company, humiliated further by the proposal that it should carry coals from Newcastle to London. The ultimate disgrace was the sale by auction at Milford Haven on 28 October

1885. A scribbled note on a copy of the 'Particulars and Conditions of Sale' indicates that the contents and scrap iron fetched a total of £26,200. The contents included all the possessions of the cabins, from the staterooms to those of the crew: washbasins, looking-glasses, soap trays, cushions, and gilt chandeliers for the Ladies Saloon. The Cabin Bar had racks for hundreds of bottles; and the Chief Engineer's Cabin contained one looking-glass, one cushion, one filter, one hot-water pot, one officers' WC, and one bath for screw engineers. While alive, *The Great Eastern* had class; in death, as the 22,927 tons of metal were dismantled for scrap (the *Canberra* is 45,000 tons), the skeletons of several workmen were found imprisoned within the iron walls. The great ship had been jinxed from the outset, as if it had been cursed by the unfortunate builders as they suffocated.

By 1900 the atmosphere on the island had improved so drastically that Walter Besant was able to describe it as 'a place where one might deliberately choose to be born, because, apart from the general well-being of the people and healthfulness of the air, there is a spirit of enterprise imbibed by every boy who grows up in this admirable island ... There are no slums ... I have never seen any hooligans ... you will not see any drunken men nor beggars, nor any signs of misery.' As one of the docks was known locally as 'Drunken Dock' this sounds like a case of romantic licence.

Indeed, pub life in those earlier days was so boisterous that drunks were frequently strapped to stretcher-like carts and wheeled to the nearest police station. 'The Black Maria,' someone told me, 'has done away with a lot of excitement.'

Now it seemed an area forgotten by the rest of London, which added to my sympathy towards it. In those first months I never tired of turning the corner from the Newcastle Arms to the small Park of the Isles on the water's edge with the glass dome which led to the foot tunnel, emerging next to the Cutty Sark at Greenwich on the other side. After the turmoil of Commercial Road, the island had tranquillity. The roads were wider, with large empty spaces, parks and playing fields. I crossed bridges, walked past high walls that were dwarfed by even higher ships and through streets named after girls – Sophia Street, Maria Street – or the Indies – Havannah Street, Cuba Street – or after ships – Barque Street and Schooner Street. Millwall and Blackwall were named after the great walls that kept back the floods, and the mills that once stood there.

My mind made up, I was determined to take over the Newcastle Arms. I contacted the brokers, who put me in touch with the brewers' district manager, who referred me, doubtfully, to his superiors at Head Office. They were surprised, sceptical and suddenly charming as they realised their extraordinary luck in finding someone so naive. Their books, which were their bibles, told them unequivocally that the Newcastle Arms was moribund.

Why disillusion me? Yet one man had the decency to ask if I realised the risk that I was embarking on. I replied complacently that I should hardly be risking my money if I thought I was going to fail. At least they had warned me, and after my ill-conceived boast they went into conference and emerged spluttering with smiles and the admission that my name as an alleged 'TV Personality' could prove an attraction, like that of a champion boxer who ends up behind the bar. And I had plenty of experience in front of it.

Usually the applicants are a married couple for the post of manager, brow-beaten and patronised by the brewers with their sadistic use of power; but I was after a tenancy and I was damned if I was going to appear subservient. Disconcerted by such independence, they raised no objection when I told them that the name of their pub was ridiculous – 'The Newcastle Arms, on the Isle of Dogs! How did it get such a name in the first place?' Unless proverbial coals from Newcastle had landed here, but they asked if I had an alternative in mind.

The Waterman's Arms (formerly the Newcastle Arms) seen from the water by Dick Whyte

'Yes. The Waterman's Arms.' It seemed only right to name it after my home on the bend of the river, once a small waterfront pub and evening refuge.

They were unaware of this nostalgia and though it involved considerable paperwork, they agreed. Within a few days the deal was on. I paid a deposit and a temporary licence was granted. In far-off Western Australia where I was not forgiven for describing Kalgoorlie on television as 'the most godforsaken spot on earth', the *Commerce-Industrial and Mining Review* greeted the news with the acid comment: 'It is interesting that Mr Farson has reached his level in a cockney pub.'

With the wheels in motion I became a publican before I scarcely knew it. This involved a 'going-in' fee and rent, and the agreement that I would pay the brewers for all the beer and spirits I ordered and keep any profit after my overheads. I skipped ahead.

'If only' are two of the saddest words in the language, and as I am a fatalist I try to ignore them, though they stick like burrs. *If* I had been able to resort to the expert advice of a business partner, intelligent bank manager, or trusted accountant, the next few years would have been different, though I have no idea if they would have been better. A partner might have realised the potential value of the Newcastle as a freehold property, for no one else had shown the slightest interest in taking it over and the brewers might have rid themselves of such an albatross if the bargaining had been sufficiently tough.

It was a spacious building with a large room upstairs and high windows from the floor to the ceiling, one of which gave a sideways glance at the river. There was ample accommodation; spacious and gracious too. Why this impressive house was situated at the top of this remote slipway remains a mystery. Judging by the space downstairs, it had been conceived as a public house, possibly as a complement to Greenwich which lay opposite, at a time when the river was full of traffic.

Though I discovered so much about my home in Limehouse, that first surge of curiosity had gone and I failed to trace the background to the pub I had taken over.

Far from taking advantage of this wealth of space, there was no question of my leaving Narrow Street to live there. Without realising how self-defeating this would be, I had no wish to live above such noisy premises. Consequently I needed a manager, or, as it turned out, a series of managers.

When I appeared at the autumn Brewster Sessions in 1962 for the full licence, my heart paused as the magistrates asked the police if there was any objection, and the unexpected reply was 'Yes!' The brewers' solicitor who told me there would be no problem looked aghast, but apparently something was 'known' against the manager who stood beside me, an old friend whose background seemed impeccable. I cast him an apprehensive look, wondering if the crime was violence, rape or fraud. It proved to be 'larceny' – the theft of a beer mug in Portsmouth a decade or so earlier when he was in the Royal Navy. The magistrates indulged in magisterial titter, and I laughed too, with relief, though I wondered how something so trivial could have stayed on the books for so long. The licence was granted.

There is no denying that the brewers did me proud in their transformation of the Newcastle into the Waterman's Arms. I was tied to them with a vengeance but they were responsible for all the alterations to the 'fixtures and fittings'; the incoming manager had no say in the matter, but as the tenant I had to pay for the new furniture and the ubiquitous 'fittings', while they paid for the structural work, so I was determined to have my say and the brewers proved surprisingly sympathetic to my ideas.

They chose the perfect architect, Roddy Gradidge, a man who actually used his eyes and his imagination instead of restricting his outlook to the drawing-board. Years later, on Dartmoor, we stopped at an ancient pub which the brewers had asked him to look at, because the new tenants wanted to 'modernise' it, and it was plain that they thought wistfully in terms of formica and fruit machines. Looking around him, Roderick Gradidge announced his decision: 'Do absolutely nothing to this wonderful place. To change a thing would be a crime.' With the Waterman's, however, he was able to create a fun-palace out of a place that was dead and dreary.

Ebullient, enthusiastic, ear-ringed, Roddy Gradidge tried so hard to be an eccentric that once he abandoned the attempt he became one. Today, now that a ring in a man's ear is commonplace, he sports a ponytail and kilt which enhance his startling, portly figure and distract from his formidable talent.

Roddy Gradidge is one of the few in his profession to retain his independence. He is noted for his unsentimental devotion to Victorian design, his book on Lutyens, and his conversion of a tiny, disused station in Staffordshire into homes for the Landmark Trust, with grander designs on St Pancras: 'the original hotel by Gilbert Scott in the 1860s is still there, behind the plaster-board.' Concentrating on work he likes, he transformed a Gothic mansion for one of the Beatles, added an orangery to Cholmondeley Castle, and assembled an Edwardian street around the Tramway Museum at Crich in Derbyshire, for the trams to run through. Probably his greatest triumph is the conversion of a girls' school at Bodelwyddan Castle in Wales to the Welsh National Portrait Gallery, with Victorian furniture, wallpaper and statuary to enhance the paintings – a bold concept which attracted 60,000 visitors in the first year and won the National Heritage Museum of the Year in 1989.

That lay ahead. When he was chosen as the designer for the new Waterman's I was exceptionally fortunate, while for him it was a rare opportunity.

Working together, we conceived the upper level as a 'public' bar related to the Thames near by. The dividing wall was replaced by several arches so that I could look down on a stage, exactly as I hoped.

Music Hall had become my passion ever since I discovered the Last Night at the Metropolitan in the Edgware Road, which was due for demolition to provide space for a new motorway. It proved the first of many 'last nights'; eventually it was discovered that this was a slip of the planner's pen and totally unnecessary, but this came too late. The day the Met was demolished I arrived with permission to rescue what I could as the Music Hall came tumbling down around me. The front of a box and two supporting caryatids became part of the upstairs bar at the Waterman's. I also bid grandiloquently at the auction of the old Collins Music Hall at Islington for a splendid pastel of Harry Tate by the Edwardian caricaturist Ospovat, and a large portrait of Little Tich, who was named as a minuscule contrast to the massive Tichborne Claimant.

Don Ross, the widower of Gertie Gitana whose famous song was 'Nellie Dean', gave me a handsome red and white poster advertising Marie Lloyd on her final bill, and I collected more Music Hall material from the shops in Cecil Court off St Martin's Lane, adding to my own extensive collection of Victorian and Edwardian song-sheet covers. Friends in showbusiness sent me signed photographs – a mixed bag including Joe Brown, Peter Finch, Trevor Howard, Lionel Bart and Richard Dimbleby – and these were duly mounted and framed.

On a visit to Liverpool I saw a superb example of illustrated glass in a small pub, rising six feet high, of Britannia flanked by wheat, sheaves of corn and flowers.

'God, that's beautiful!' I exclaimed.

'Yes,' agreed the landlord. 'Pity it's got to be smashed,' explaining that the pub was due to be demolished the following week. I bought the glass on the spot, paying even more to have it transported. I expected a pantechnicon on the day of its arrival, but a van unloaded twenty small packing cases and it took me thirty seconds before the awful truth dawned: they had sent me the panels of stained glass, garishly depicting a scene from the Bible, which lined the pub's corridor. I raced to the phone.

'Mistake? Britannia? Oh, the glass. We broke *that* yesterday!'

My collection of Music Hall was balanced in the public bar by old prints of the East End and the docks which were hung against brown parcel wallpaper, in preference to an art nouveau design which Gradidge had rediscovered in an old Sanderson's book which was sent upstairs instead. There were old engravings of Greenwich, early topographical plans for the West India Docks, a panoramic view of the Thames that stretched for several feet, and a colourful scene of Greenwich painted especially by Dick Whyte, who excelled himself.

My joy in acquiring the collection was tempered by the dismal spectacle of draped dust sheets as the builders moved in to make the structural alterations. Gradidge warned me that when they were finished I would be shocked by the blood-red paint we had agreed on for the saloon, which was just as well for when I saw the walls for the first time I reeled back from their impact. But when the posters and decorations were up, they provided an aggressive though striking background.

We had two openings. The first was farcical, with half the pub cordoned off for the builders. A week earlier I had to go into hospital for the removal of a growth, which proved non-malignant. I was lying in bed afterwards thinking how fortunate it was that I had kept the opening night secret, when Queenie came to visit me.

'I thought you ought to know, dear,' she said, 'that everyone is going to your opening.'

'Everyone?'

'Everyone in the East End – you know how word gets around.'

'But we've told nobody,' I said. 'Do they expect free drinks?'

'Well, dear, they do rather expect a drink on the house.'

I was so unfamiliar with pub protocol that I decided to serve free bits of food instead and hired Chinese waiters from the fashionable Lotus House in the Edgware Road. Queenie looked at me askance, started to say something, and stopped.

Earlier that day, I arrived at the old Newcastle with a stick, straight from the London Clinic, to find the brokers with little piles of money on the tables in front of them as they valued the sticks of furniture and remaining stock, usually a substantial item but no more than a few 'empties' in the case of the 'pub with no beer'.

The departing landlord shook my hand gratefully for I had saved him from impending prosecution by the brewers for debt, and he left with the broadest grin I had ever seen. For a brief moment I wondered why he was so relieved, shook my head, and forgot all about it as I signed a cheque to the brewers of just over £1,000, the largest of my life. Then I pulled my first pint as the landlord of the Waterman's Arms.

Billy Walker, and the playwright Alun Owen, turned up to join me, presumably in expectation of a house-warming party after my invitation, only to find the place empty apart from the builders and a journalist from the *Daily Mirror*. They concealed their disappointment and I was too preoccupied to notice.

The afternoon passed quietly as I coped with the 'reps', ordering glasses, cigarettes for the new machines, and various gadgets which I was assured would prove indispensable. Deliveries arrived belatedly and the manager and the new staff struggled with the barrels and learnt how to attach them in the cool cellars below. Queenie and Slim Watts had allowed me to work briefly behind the bar at the Ironbridge in an attempt to teach me the basic tricks of the business, though their customers complained that I was slow and I still had much to learn.

Tired and dusty, I limped back to Narrow Street for a shower and returned at opening time to brace myself against the deluge at opening time.

Nothing happened. After ten minutes a local resident peered inside and went out again. Returning a few minutes later with his wife, he grabbed my shoulder and whirled me around to face the wall: '*The Great Eastern* was launched around that corner – and it sank!' Grateful for their custom I poured them Guinness on the house. Another aged couple came in, as they did nightly for the next few years, for these were our 'regulars' – all of them. Occasional strangers wandered in and out. The silence was so deafening that rather than meet the eyes of the staff I retreated to the kitchen to nibble a pancake roll under the impassive scrutiny of the Chinese waiters. At least it was impossible to know what *they* were thinking.

And then, at eight o'clock, as they were to do so often, the doors were pushed apart and a torrent of people started to pour inside. Within a few minutes the pub was full. A customer jumped on stage and played the piano, Queenie seized both the opportunity and the microphone, and the Chinese waiters from the Lotus House emerged, grinning, with their trays held high. This absurd, extravagant gesture was interpreted as something different and was well received.

In spite of the dust sheets, the chaos and my own dreadful amateurism, this was one of the better nights for the simple reason that this was an East End occasion unalloyed with slummers from 'up West'. I had suspected it before, but here was proof of the East Enders' capacity for enjoying themselves.

Generous and friendly, appreciative of the misconceived Chinese food, they created the atmosphere I had been hoping for. The East Enders' reaction was most rewarding, for they took to the pub instinctively as a place of their own where they were welcome to participate.

When closing time came too early, with the tyrannical licensing laws of the day, I removed some 'Keep Britain White' stickers from the Gents, and went over to a barman who was having difficulty in persuading the last customer to leave. He was a tough-looking character, but I was in a state of confident euphoria. Remembering the times that Gaston had asked me to leave the old French pub under similar conditions, I used the same technique. 'Now, now,' I said unctuously, 'you know I can't serve you after hours, and the law's outside.' This was true, for several policemen were watching us intently from across the road, and may well have been expecting a drink on the house themselves. Another point of pub protocol which I never understood.

'Tell you what,' I added as if in after-thought, 'come back in the morning if you'll be so kind and have a drink with me then. Is that in order?'

'No problem,' he muttered. He shook my hand, I unbolted the door, and he shambled out like a sweet if unsteady lamb.

'There,' I said, turning to the staff who had been watching open-mouthed. 'That's how you do it.'

'Cor,' said one of the East End barmen, 'you don't half take some liberties, Dan. Know who that was?' He named a member of the most notorious gang in East London.

'Never heard of them,' I replied, which was true at the time.

We never had trouble at the Waterman's, apart from the evening when a Guards' officer and his Sloane debutante stole the microphone. An immense plate-glass window fronted the saloon and every time I walked up Glengarnock Avenue – another absurdly inappropriate name – I tensed myself in case I found it cracked or smashed to smithereens. I had no need to worry, for the window remained intact.

Undeterred by my inexperience, I ventured into areas which should have intimidated me. A 'song-plugger' I had interviewed in Denmark Street, London's tin-pan-alley, helped to find me musicians, but I soon suspected that he used the Waterman's as a graveyard for friends who were washed up and very understandably out of work. To start with our star turn was a middle-aged xylophonist. I happen to like the xylophone but this was hardly pub entertainment. The piano and local turns were a relief.

To an extent I was serving an apprenticeship, and by the time of our official opening to demonstrate the new Waterman's in all its pristine glory, we had a group of first-rate musicians who worked by day and enjoyed the fun and their modest wages at night. As I had intended, the opening coincided with the filming of *Time Gentlemen Please!* which explored the boom in East End public house entertainment, so it seemed obvious to give my own pub a boost. The TV lights, known as 'brutes', enhanced the atmosphere and revealed the skill of Roderick Gradidge. He had antagonised the staff and builders by descending on them like a sergeant major, issuing his orders as if they were on parade, but they were less antagonistic now that they saw the result. The Waterman's looked magnificent. Even my friends who had doubted my ability all along conceded their surprise.

Shirley Bassey singing in the Waterman's Arms

Time Gentlemen Please! featured our compère Kim Cordell, a larger-than-life personality with a voice that overcame the pub chatter, whom I had discovered in the Rising Sun in Mile End Road; Sulky Gowers, bald, smartly dressed in the style of Al Capone, who waved his stick dramatically as he sang 'Buddy Can You Spare a Dime'; Queenie Watts with 'Limehouse Blues'; Tommy Pudding with 'Put a bit of Treacle on Your Pudding, Mary Anne', wearing a hat and a Max Miller leer.

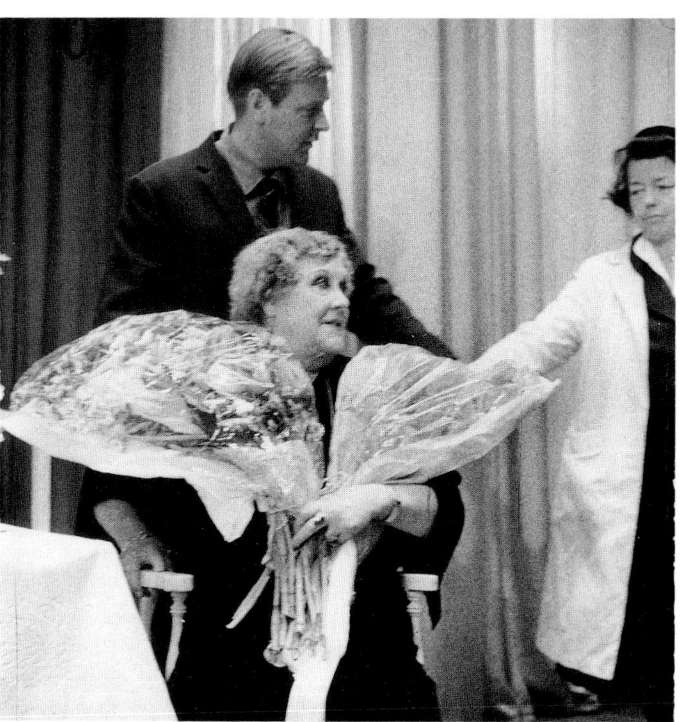

Ida Barr, myself and Joan Littlewood at Ida's last appearance at the Metropolitan Theatre, Edgware Road

These were the antidote to the usual Variety fare on television which looked synthetic by comparison. Television had not seen the likes of them before. And to emphasise that Music Hall had returned to the pubs where it began, I featured Ida Barr who sang the number she brought back from America after the First World War – 'Oh, You Beautiful Doll' – with a life-size blow-up of her then, beside her on the stage.

I had included Ida in an item for *This Week* on one of the last nights of the Metropolitan in the Edgware Road, along with G.H. Eliot, 'the Chocolate Coloured Coon' who sang 'Lily of Laguna'; Hetty King, the male impersonator with 'All the Nice Girls Love a Sailor'; and Marie Lloyd Junior who gave a spirited rendering of 'It's a Bit of a Ruin that Cromwell Knocked About a Bit', with a hint of her mother's charm, though little of her own.

Later I hired the Met for an afternoon and recorded them on an LP called *Music Hall* with embarrassing introductions from myself which make me wince when I hear them today: 'And now we have Albert Whelan, still going strong at the age of eighty-five having thankfully recovered from the recent operation in which he lost his leg. He is *still* whistling his famous signature tune...'

They were a gallant band of survivors. G.H. Eliot was so beautifully mannered that it was easy to understand why he was such a matinée idol in his day. Ida Barr became a close friend, easy to visit in her tiny tenement flat off Charing Cross Road which she had decorated like a country cottage. Unlike Hetty King who had saved her money with shrewd investments, Ida had nothing, though when I introduced her to Joan Littlewood, Joan remarked, 'I think you're the richest woman I have met.' Consequently, Ida relished her new-found fame and the treats it brought to her life. A warm-hearted, cheerful woman she lived up to her hoary joke – 'I may not be a spring chicken, but I'm still game!' – and she was hugely popular.

Unlike modern 'artistes' who repeated the old numbers with burbling jollity, it was Ida's strength, and that of G.H. Eliot and Hetty King, that they sang the words with passionate conviction. 'Oh, You Beautiful Doll' was a love song which began confidentially, as she virtually beckoned the audience towards her:

> Honey dear,
> Listen here,
> Just turn out the light
> And then come over here.
> Nestle close up to my side
> My heart's a-fire
> With love's desire.

And *then* into the rousing, familiar chorus: 'Oh, You Beautiful Doll!'

Ida typified the vigour of Music Hall. At the age of fifteen she ran away to Ireland to join a pantomime chorus under the name of Maud Laverne, which she thought was 'posh', just as Marie Lloyd had chosen Bella Delmere. Ida weighed thirteen stone, seven pounds – 'They liked a lot of woman in those days' – and the photograph taken of her next year when she was sixteen, with an embroidered shamrock on her bust, shows that she was exquisite.

In 1910 she ran off to America to get away from her husband, an ill-tempered comedian called Gus Harris – 'The only Yiddisher Scotsman in the Irish Fusiliers' – and she returned with 'Beautiful Doll' and the latest rag-time dance 'Everybody's Doing it Now'. Soon she was off again to South Africa and then to Australia with a new, typical number – 'STOP, STOP, STOP ... don't you *dare* to stop, come over and love me some more'.

The managements asked her to stay in Australia but she turned them down: 'They all knew I was in love with a feller in South Africa; I'd have gone there if I'd had to travel by cattle-boat.' So they gave her a farewell presentation of a carved boomerang and a plaque.

'What happened to the man in South Africa?'

For once the big eyes saddened. 'He died. Oh, well, I was never lucky in love.' The smile returned: 'In those days it was the old ones who were after me, now it seems to be the young fellows like yourself.'

It was Ida who kindled my obsession with Music Hall, showing me that the myth surrounding it was less interesting than the truth, and Marie Lloyd more monstrous than the whitewash. Ida even had a good word to say for her third husband Bernard Dillon: 'People say he lived off her; they forget they ran through his money first. If she threw things at him – well, you can't expect a man to take that.'

After Marie's funeral, when Dillon was forbidden to join the sisters in his former living-room, Ida sat with him in the kitchen until he was told that he had been left out of the will, when he took his hat and left.

I enjoyed the filming for *Time Gentlemen Please!* Rollo Gamble always added a zest to the occasion and made the performers feel important, which brought out the best in them. I thought the programme looked attractive, with no idea of the impact it would make.

Queenie Watts being filmed singing 'Limehouse Blues' on the slip next to the Waterman's Arms

Slightly disconsolate the next morning, for 92 Narrow Street had been burgled, presumably by thieves who thought the programme was going out live and that I was incarcerated in a distant studio instead of in the Waterman's, I opened the newspapers on the bus to Aldwych in case it had been reviewed. I caught my breath.

> CHEERS – TO UNCORKED VARIETY – streets ahead of the polished 'Hippodrome' – side-streets perhaps, but better television. *The Daily Mirror*

> CHEERS, I SAY FOR THIS BOUNCING FUN AT THE BAR – The wheel has come full-circle, for music-hall was born in the bar and moved out into the theatre. Now it is dead and its roisterous, bawdy, irresistible spirit has gone back whence it came ... caught the enveloping friendliness of the atmosphere to perfection. *The Daily Mail*

> LET US SEE US MORE OFTEN – the best pub crawl the sober little screen has ever witnessed. This programme gave us an all too rare chance to balance the mid-Atlantic idioms of a wholly contrived pop world with the rougher nuggets of a half-forgotten and older kind of tradition. Perhaps the greatest pleasure was communicated from the gallery of faces listening, drinking and chattering at the crowded little tables. When Ida Barr, the magnificent old-timer from the abandoned music halls sang 'Oh, You Beautiful Doll', the cacophony of pint-chinks and chair-screech died down in a moment of the former magic. Dennis Potter [no less], *Daily Herald*

15

Time Gentlemen Please!

IF ALL THIS sounds nauseatingly happy, rest assured: the rapids lay ahead in all their treachery. Meanwhile, the period of abeyance was over. Suddenly the Waterman's was the place to visit, and West Enders descended *en masse*, dressed down for the occasion in headscarves and jeans.

'POW!' exclaimed a centre-spread in the *Sunday Mirror* on so-called 'Swinging London': 'So this is what really goes on in our great FUSED capital.'

God help me! I had created an 'in' place, though I was less appalled by trendiness than I would be today.

My Visitors' Book filled up with unlikely names: Emlyn Williams; Francis Bacon, who came with William Burroughs, Alexander Trocchi and Michael Portman; George Melly; and Harry Carpenter – all on one page. Clint Eastwood is on his own on the final page, with 'Rowdy' scrawled underneath, a part he was playing at the time.

Joan Littlewood – 'What a swish pub!' she wrote reprovingly – brought Jacques Tati who offered me a part in his next film, which I accepted and then heard nothing more; impresarios, Lord Delfont and David Merrick; Claudette Colbert; Groucho Marx; George Martin; Lionel Bart; Montagu of Beaulieu; Lord Boothby; Alan Bates; Shirley Anne Field; Sandy Mackendrick, who directed *Whisky Galore*; Trevor Howard; Peter Shaffer; Ken Tynan ... the list goes on, for the celebrities found a degree of anonymity.

There were nights when I did achieve a new sort of Music Hall, with acts ranging from our pop-group Karl King and the Vendettas (Karl was only fourteen) to Ida Barr. George Melly and Annie Ross were never too grand to take part, sometimes together with their duet of Frankie and Johnny. Annie brought such friends as Sarah Vaughan and Tony Bennett.

(Left to right) myself, the late Sean Lynch, his wife Annie Ross and Tony Bennett

The local talent delighted the audience with the unpredictability of a man who sang 'Mule Train' and banged his head with a tin tray to the music; a docker who impersonated Frankenstein's monster; the taxi-driver from the Rising Sun who sang Al Jolson; and a girl in spectacles, dressed with the severity of a City secretary, who was known as the 'white mouse' and sang so startlingly off-key that she was greeted with cheers whenever she appeared.

I indulged myself with lavish parties in the room upstairs, after the entertainment below. On one occasion Christabel Aberconway sat next to one of the arches and waved to the populace below like the Queen Mother, while her rival, Diana Cooper was determined to stand in the public bar throughout, though she must have been eighty. Writing about the evening in the *New Statesman*, Anthony Carson said, 'You could feel it was a river party. Beauty, absolutely authentic, was suddenly provided by Lady Diana Cooper; she made you stop still in your tracks. Lovely Far Eastern girls served Indonesian dishes, [actually Mrs Farmer's Eurasian daughters from the Old Friends] the sampans weren't far away, all passengers were going ashore, please, Joseph Conrad and W.W. Jacobs were coming up the gangplank.'

When I told Diana Cooper that a number of people had praised her beauty, she corrected me sharpishly: 'I much prefer *pretty*', and that was the more accurate.

Eric Crabtree, a power in the fashion world, held a party one evening with such guests as Hardy Amies, Barbara Goalen, Mary Quant and Norman Hartnell with his arm in a sling. David Jacobs, the showbusiness solicitor who could not resist a party, also came, along with Shirley Bassey, who was persuaded to sing 'I Who Have Nothing' with the irony that she was plainly pregnant. This happened to be a favourite number of Kim Cordell's and the group surprised her with their backing. The East End crowd who mingled with the celebrities relished the glamour and listened to her in absolute silence.

Brian Epstein made the effort to return to the pub in order to hear Karl King and the Vendettas, whom I was promoting in the vain hope that he might see them as potential Beatles. As bad luck would have it, Karl was ill that night, our usual group were booked elsewhere, and I made the mistake of contacting my friend in tin-pan-alley who promised to send a last-minute substitute. He must have been the oldest, saddest musician in the business, or long since out of it, who sat by the piano with the lugubrious grimace of a dyspeptic toad. Epstein vanished, never to return, and Julian Slade signed the Visitors' Book with the comment: 'Shoot the pianist.'

The interior of the Waterman's Arms (photograph by Peter Botton)

After her party at the Boltons, I arranged a party for Judy Garland with the assistance of Burt Shevelove, author of *A Funny Thing Happened on the Way to the Forum* and possessor of a brilliant, New York Jewish wit. Garland was so unaffected that I had not realised the extent of her Hollywood stardom, though I took the precaution of warning the staff to say nothing about her arrival. This spread the word immediately and I was dismayed to approach the pub and find Glengarnock Avenue filled with hundreds of East Enders. Knowing how fragile she had become, as skeletal as a quail, I arranged for an escort to prevent her from being hurt in the crush. I need not have worried, for when she arrived, an hour late as usual, the crowd gasped audibly as they saw her fragility and made way for her instinctively, clapping her arrival.

Judy Garland was nicer than her reputation: friendly throughout, attentive to Ida Barr though she had little idea who she was, chatting on the balcony that overlooked the river, for this proved the hottest night of the year.

After closing time, when the pub was empty, she announced that she wanted to sing. My new manager, however, told her it was against the law to turn on the lights in the saloon. This was a case of bloody-mindedness, and I told him I would be happy to pay if we were fined.

'No,' said Garland, 'I'll pay.'

Finally, she sang by the moonlight seeping from the river and the reflection from the street lights opposite, as a guest played the opening notes of 'Come Rain or Come Shine'. Garland listened attentively – a click of her fingers, and she was away, with that extraordinary ecstasy that was hers alone, though many have tried to recapture it. Her only complaint was the absence of any photographer, for I had been scrupulous in keeping the press at bay, unaware of her addiction to publicity.

Looking back, I doubt if I was fully aware of the trend I began, for I remember my surprise when Colin MacInnes came to the Waterman's and advised me to become an 'impresario', actually giving me a copy of a musical he had written with a Music Hall theme, called *The Boy in the Gallery* after the song that Marie Lloyd pinched from Nelly Power.

Outwardly the most curmudgeonly of men, Colin shared my interest both in Music Hall and in the East End, for he had lived in Spitalfields for two years as he wrote in his weekly page in *New Society* –

> with Nicholas Hawksmoor's splendidly baroque Christ Church rising before my window, and the unspoiled Huguenot glories of Fournier Street standing beyond, the area rivals any of the capital. Humanly, it is cosmopolitan, vivacious, elegant (in the truest sense), and informal. The streets were alive and their inhabitants accessible. You could also eat and drink there round the clock, which you can't do in London, West, unless you're loaded.

Because we had so much in common, he might have resented me as a rival, especially as he yearned for greater recognition for his books, such as *Absolute Beginners*. Yet the account of his visit to the Waterman's Arms could not have been more generous, especially welcome from such a fine writer:

> Most of us have fantasies we fail to bend into realities, but Mr Dan Farson has – to coin a phrase – made his dream come true. This was to be a publican in the far East End of London . . .
>
> And not content with realizing his own dream, Mr Farson has realized one of mine: which is that popular song and entertainment should evade the telly screens and radio to which they have been banished from the few surviving Theatres of Variety and reappear, as they did in their days of authenticity and glory, on a performer-to-audience basis where there is direct, personal communication . . .
>
> I must confess that, on a first recent visit to the Waterman's Arms, I went with pre-packaged scorn and trepidation. I expected a tarted-up 'East End' pub for sensation-seeking westerners (like the Prospect of Thing, whose name I must not mention, and which has long been ruined by its expatriate clientele), and I anticipated the acts would all be corny. Quite, quite wrong. The decor hits just the right note of understanding nostalgia, the acts are excellent, ranging – rightly – from the traditional to the furiously up-to-date, and the most startlingly delightful element is the public.
>
> I wrote earlier of East End elegance. This may sound incredible if you associate this quantity automatically with London SW3, yet I believe if you want to see a sharp, sexy, relaxed yet astringent public – if you'd like to observe a *chic* that isn't off the peg and by-passes the bogus glamour of the advertising agencies – you'll find these best in Mr Farson's pub or those he featured on his programme.

Coming from Colin MacInnes, this was a rare gesture of goodwill.

Perhaps this is the moment when I should cry 'Cut!', and end with success, for in spite of my wretched naivety, I had fulfilled my objective of creating a popular entertainment pub in the heart of the East End, reflecting the bravura of the cockneys. In a guide to public houses published soon afterwards, the Waterman's Arms gained more references in the index than any other pub in Britain, and considerably more than the fashionable 'Prospect of Thing' (as MacInnes called the Prospect of Whitby) further up the river.

I began to notice warning signals. Walking up Glengarnock Avenue from the bus stop around the corner, I saw one of the bar managers drive up in a smart new car, and realised, vaguely, that the staff looked more affluent every day.

It was disconcerting to learn that though Queenie and Slim Watts lived on the premises at the Ironbridge, they were being robbed consistently. After several months, while friends kept careful watch, they discovered that their assistant manager had been cheating them, which made them particularly bitter as they had been grooming him to take over now that Queenie's career as an actress had been established.

If Queenie and Slim were cheated with all their experience, I was a natural victim of the numerous pub 'fiddles' which are so easy to practise yet so hard to detect. However, these were comparatively trivial, and I believe, or like to believe, that the staff were reasonably honest.

As for their accountant, who had become mine, I know he was inadequate in his lack of advice and I suspect that he was crooked though outwardly pin-striped and meticulous. He revealed a nasty streak when he presented his account to Queenie Watts at a low moment a few years later, when she asked for time to pay. Regarding him as one of her closest friends, it came as a shock when he replied: 'No. But you can give me your wedding ring instead,' making a gesture as if she should take it off on the spot.

He is dead now, his last years enriched by a considerable fortune, a Rolls Royce, a house in the country and other luxuries, though it turned out that some of these had not been paid for.

He confided to me once that his life had changed completely because of the Waterman's Arms, and I can well believe it.

But the real failure was more basic and ironic – I was too successful.

On the way to nowhere in a non-residential district, nothing happened at the Waterman's until eight o'clock and then it was so crowded that I overheard people complaining, as they squeezed inside, that it was impossible to reach the bar; so they would listen for a few minutes and move on to another pub where they could get a drink more easily.

The pubs along the way to mine benefited from the bonanza, particularly the City Arms which specialised in 'drag'. I stopped there myself one evening to hear people asking if this was the pub run by Dan Farson. 'Yes,' they were told.

Everyone else prospered. Today, when East End pubs continue after midnight with the excuse of entertainment or the tacit approval of the police, I could charge an entrance fee, but in those days this was illegal and the licensing laws demanded that the pub close at 11.00 p.m.

The wages for the entertainers, even the breakage of a couple of beer mugs, could not be covered within such a limited time. My life became a sham as friends elbowed their way into the bar and congratulated me on the money I must be making.

One morning as I lay in bed in Narrow Street, the bank manager phoned to warn me that my business account was £3,000 overdrawn, so what was I going to do about it? I told him to sell the remaining shares left me by my parents, and I gave in my notice to the brewers. This was when I was most in need of advice, but it was not forthcoming. Later – far too late to be of any practical use – the bank manager told me I should have gone bankrupt, but such a step did not occur to me. I should have fought it out with the brewers. I had earned them hundreds of thousands of pounds but this was small beer compared to the gigantic goodwill of *Time Gentlemen Please!* and the attention I had drawn to pub entertainment in the East End, an advertising agency's dream worth millions.

Instead, I experienced the power of the brewers as they exacted their due, insisting on a year's notice unless they found a new tenant prepared to pay the going-in fee of £4,500 which they demanded for the Waterman's reputation.

(Left) Francis Bacon and the Lady Rose MacLaren. (Below) Virginia Law, Sir Robert Helpmann, the Lady Rose MacLaren and Mick Donaldson, first manager of the Waterman's Arms

Now I appreciated the dilemma of my predecessor, forced to stay against his will. Week after week, cheque book after cheque book, I paid for my losses as pointlessly as throwing money into the Thames. Prospective tenants had a look, and were never heard of again. It was true that the Isle of Dogs was still a moribund area and the sum demanded by the brewers was unrealistic; but I learnt later that a member of the staff discouraged every applicant in the hope that he would be asked to become the manager. To make it even more lunatic, the brewers asked me to apply for a new licence, though the police came to my rescue inadvertently with hints that they might oppose it.

At last I came to my senses with the discovery that I could browbeat the brewers at their own game. They, and not the law, insisted on opening hours and prices, but provided they were within licensing hours I could open when I liked. I shut the pub all day, opening at eight in the evening when I served no draught beer and doubled the prices. For two revelatory weeks I ran the Waterman's myself and there were no complaints apart from the brewers' rep. As the Waterman's showed a profit at last, I was tempted to continue, but when a prospective tenant was secured I was thankful to leave.

Soon I faced the ritual of the changeover with the piles of cash and haggling over furniture and stock, so exciting a few years earlier, so dismal now. I shook hands with my successor and I did not envy him.

Shortly afterwards I met Robert Carrier, who had started a new restaurant. He pointed to his waistline: 'I've lost twelve pounds.'

'That's nothing,' I replied, 'I've lost £12,000.' But it proved far more than that in the end, and, worst of all, involved the sale of my paintings in order to honour my debt.

I told myself then, and many times since, that I would rather lose my money on such a venture than be wiped out overnight in a stock-exchange deal. At least I was left with the memories of the good times, especially the extensions at Christmas and New Year when the East Enders joined in with the old songs and a genuine knees-up and the Waterman's belonged to them.

As for *Time Gentlemen Please!*, even that success rebounded. It entered the top ten ratings at Number Seven, and though we had never met I received a letter from Leslie Grade, the managing director of the Grade Organisation: 'May I just drop you this note to congratulate you on one of the best television shows I have ever seen.'

Maurice Wiggins in the *Sunday Times* confirmed my new resolve:

> Mr Farson has some good things to say, such as 'The West End has never been so hollow and tawdry – I am always glad to go to East, to the real vitality and warmth and *elegance* where the pubs really welcome you.' His long love-affair with the East End is a fortunate thing for television. In this new venture he is mining a rich vein of ore; if it doesn't give out, he may well find himself setting a fashion.

I prepared an outline for Associated Rediffusion, suggesting that we followed up with a series which showed real people in real places in other parts of Britain such as Liverpool where there was new, vibrant talent. Instead, AR asked Rollo Gamble to produce a series in the studio using such East End stars as Kim Cordell and Ray Martine, and he agreed.

I might have done the same, but this ended a happy collaboration between us and though Rollo added his inimitable zest, *Stars and Garters* was the negation of spontaneity as extras sipped watered tea instead of beer. The critics pounced on the difference: '*Issue Must be Faced – Fake or Reality,*' wrote Michael Gowers. 'The show was, of course, the love child of an excellent documentary about public entertainers in the East End, but with the almighty difference that it was just a fake – fake setting, fake customers, fake drink, fake conviviality.' Another critic mourned the loss of *Time Gentlemen Please!*: 'I wish Mr Farson would be returned to us, and repeat his enormously enjoyable explorations. *Stars and Garters* is a poor substitute. It doesn't smell of beer and skittles.' But the studio series put paid to any resurrection.

I devised *Nights at the Comedy*, which brought the East End artists to the West End in a production by William Donaldson, and though Kim Cordell and Mrs Shufflewick excelled, praised by Harold Hobson for timing 'her' lines as skilfully as Mussolini did his trains, there was justice in the summing-up by Fergus Cashin in the *Sketch*: 'Farson really tries – without succeeding.' And that could be the epitaph for the entire venture. Conversely, it could be argued that I was hoist by my own success.

At the end of his page in *New Society*, Colin MacInnes asked:

> Can it really be that Mr Farson has squared an impossible circle? That he can encourage, and discover, authentic popular talent, face to sweaty face with a genuine popular audience, while preventing its being absorbed into the personal ambiguity of the magic box on whose miniature screen he has himself played so lively a part? Can anything today, real and vivid, begin at the grass-roots without its being swiftly hoisted into the oblivion of Tam-ratings and statistical popularity?

Sadly, the answer was 'no'.

Acting as usual on a sudden impulse, I resigned from my successful career on television, left the pub, and soon abandoned my home on the bend of the river at Limehouse, retiring to North Devon to find out if I could write.

They say you should never go back, and 'they' are right. I returned once to the Waterman's to find that it had apparently shrunk, and I fled as if from a hostile ghost. I returned to Narrow Street to interview David Owen in the house a few doors from mine in the now fashionable stretch with property exchanging hands for extraordinary sums. Dolly Fisher and her husband had bought their property which embraced the barge-repair yard and three houses for £10,000 at an auction in 1956 though she told me 'the Guv'nor went to the sale on that eventful morning solely with the idea of buying barge yard equipment.' Now it was worth £600,000.

I was early, so I went to Booty's Wine Bar which occupies the ground floor of number 92, once so noisy with the barges repaired by day and all the passing traffic on the river, now so silent. A plaque proclaimed that I lived there, once.

I went inside with the fear of recognition, and regret for all I had lost. It might have been anywhere and when I went on to the balcony the only feature which seemed at all familiar was the shimmering water whose smell evoked those early days. I have noticed this elsewhere, that water – even a particular stretch of the sea – has a character of its own.

Going back into Narrow Street, I realised that the Buildings opposite had gone. And when I travelled to the Isle of Dogs, going there by water to the new offices of the *Daily Telegraph*, returning by the Dockland Railway, I crossed new territory and it seemed to me that the soul had gone out of it.

I had the luck to know the East End before the planners moved in, while it retained an innocence and was still inviolate.

I came to Limehouse for the place and I stayed for the people. I left because all three of us were changing and now there was nothing left. It was the end of the love affair.

I have no regrets.

Index

References in italic refer to captions to illustrations.

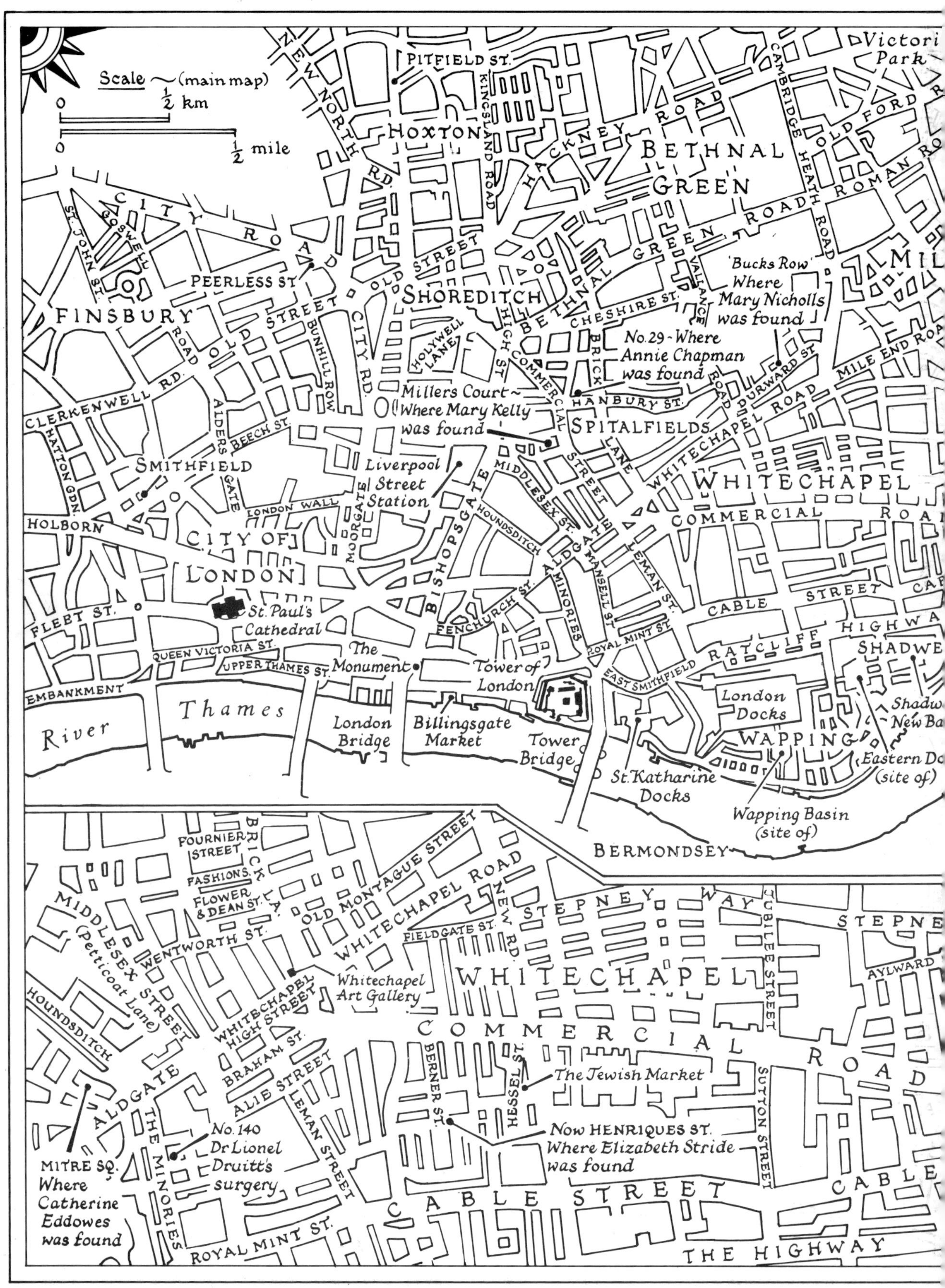
Scale ~ (main map)
0 1/2 km
0 1/2 mile
Victoria Park
PITFIELD ST.
NEW NORTH RD.
HOXTON
KINGSLAND ROAD
HACKNEY ROAD
BETHNAL GREEN
CAMBRIDGE HEATH ROAD
OLD FORD RD.
ROMAN RD.
CITY ROAD
ST. JOHN ST.
GOSWELL ROAD
PEERLESS ST.
OLD STREET
SHOREDITCH
BETHNAL GREEN ROAD
VALLANCE ROAD
'Bucks Row' Where Mary Nicholls was found
FINSBURY
BUNHILL ROW
CITY RD.
HOLYWELL LANE
HIGH ST.
COMMERCIAL ST.
CHESHIRE ST.
BRICK LANE
No.29 ~ Where Annie Chapman was found
DURWARD ST.
MILE END ROAD
CLERKENWELL RD.
HATTON GDN.
ALDERSGATE
BEECH ST.
Millers Court ~ Where Mary Kelly was found
HANBURY ST.
SPITALFIELDS
WHITECHAPEL ROAD
SMITHFIELD
Liverpool Street Station
BISHOPSGATE
MIDDLESEX ST.
WHITECHAPEL
COMMERCIAL ROAD
HOLBORN
LONDON WALL
MOORGATE
HOUNDSDITCH
ALDGATE
MANSELL ST.
LEMAN ST.
CITY OF LONDON
St. Paul's Cathedral
FLEET ST.
FENCHURCH ST.
MINORIES
CABLE STREET
ROYAL MINT ST.
HIGHWAY
RATCLIFF
SHADWELL
QUEEN VICTORIA ST.
UPPER THAMES ST.
The Monument
Tower of London
EAST SMITHFIELD
EMBANKMENT
River Thames
London Bridge
Billingsgate Market
Tower Bridge
London Docks
WAPPING
St. Katharine Docks
Wapping Basin (site of)
Eastern Dock (site of)
BERMONDSEY
FOURNIER STREET
BRICK LA.
FASHIONS
FLOWER & DEAN ST.
OLD MONTAGUE STREET
WHITECHAPEL ROAD
NEW RD.
STEPNEY WAY
JUBILEE STREET
MIDDLESEX STREET (Petticoat Lane)
WENTWORTH ST.
FIELDGATE ST.
WHITECHAPEL
Whitechapel Art Gallery
WHITECHAPEL HIGH STREET
AYLWARD
HOUNDSDITCH
BRAHAM ST.
COMMERCIAL ROAD
BERNER ST.
HESSEL ST.
The Jewish Market
SUTTON STREET
ALDGATE
ALIE STREET
LEMAN STREET
No.140 Dr Lionel Druitt's surgery
Now HENRIQUES ST. Where Elizabeth Stride was found
MITRE SQ. Where Catherine Eddowes was found
THE MINORIES
CABLE STREET
ROYAL MINT ST.
THE HIGHWAY